Wild
Mind

Other Bantam books by Natalie Goldberg:

LONG QUIET HIGHWAY:
WAKING UP IN AMERICA

BANANA ROSE: A NOVEL

CHICKEN AND IN LOVE

Wild Mind

Living the Writer's Life

NATALIE GOLDBERG

BANTAM BOOKS

NEW YORK · TORONTO · LONDON · SYDNEY · AUCKLAND

A BANTAM TRADE PAPERBACK

WILD MIND: LIVING THE WRITER'S LIFE
A Bantam Book / November 1990

*Bantam New Age and the accompanying figure design as well as the
statement "a search for meaning, growth and change" are trademarks of
Bantam Books.*

Cover painting, "Express Cafe," by
Natalie Goldberg, from the
collection of Beverly and John Rollwagen.

Library of Congress Cataloging-in-Publication Data

Goldberg, Natalie.
Wild mind: living the writer's life / Natalie Goldberg.
p. cm.
ISBN 0-553-34775-6
*1. Goldberg, Natalie—Biography. 2. Authors, American—20th
century—Biography. 3. Authorship. I. Title.*
PS3557.O3583Z478 1990
808'.042-dc20   90-519
CIP

Published simultaneously in the United States and Canada

**Bantam Books are published by Bantam Books, a division of Bantam
Doubleday Dell Publishing Group, Inc. Its trademark, consisting of the
words "Bantam Books" and the portrayal of a rooster, is Registered in U.S.
Patent and Trademark Office and in other countries. Marca Registrada.
Bantam Books, 1540 Broadway, New York, New York 10036.**

PRINTED IN THE UNITED STATES OF AMERICA

OPM   20 19 18 17 16 15

For Virginia Maclovia,
my old Talpa friend

and Carol Soutor,
my traveling partner

Acknowledgments

I wish to thank Jan Best, who typed the manuscript from the original handwritten pages; Pat Sargent, my therapist, for the great work we've done together over the last three years; Christine Saunders, my acupuncturist; Jonathon Lazear, my agent; and Toni Burbank, my editor.

Contents

viii   *Contents*

Introduction

*L*ife is not orderly. No matter how we try to make life so, right in the middle of it we die, lose a leg, fall in love, drop a jar of applesauce. In summer, we work hard to make a tidy garden, bordered by pansies with rows or clumps of columbine, petunias, bleeding hearts. Then we find ourselves longing for the forest, where everything has the appearance of disorder; yet, we feel peaceful there.

What writing practice, like Zen practice, does is bring you back to the natural state of mind, the wilderness of your mind where there are no refined rows of gladiolas. The mind is raw, full of energy, alive and hungry. It does not think in the way we were brought up to think—well-mannered, congenial.

When I finished *Writing Down the Bones* and people in my workshops read it, I thought I would not have to say anything else. I felt embarrassed to say, "Steve, you ought to be more specific there." I thought he would retort, "We know. You already told us in chapter eight." I thought I would be redundant, but reading a book about writing is different from actually getting down and doing writing. I was naïve. I should have remembered that after I read the *Tibetan Book of the Dead*, I was still afraid to die.

A book about writing isn't enough. Being a writer is a whole way of life, a way of seeing, thinking, being. It's the passing on of a lineage. Writers hand on what they know. Most of what I learned about Zen was transmitted to me through being in the presence of Katagiri Roshi, the Zen master with whom I studied.

I will give you an example. I had just moved to Minneapolis and I wanted to study Buddhism. Before I moved there, I lived in Boulder and studied with a Tibetan teacher. There was a lot of pomp and circumstance in this Tibetan tradition. It was a big center; we had to wait several months to have an interview with the teacher and we dressed up to see him.

In Minneapolis, I called the Zen center and asked if I could schedule an interview with the Zen master there. The man on the other end of the phone had a heavy Japanese accent. He told me to come right over. I realized he was the Zen master. I dressed up and ran over. Katagiri Roshi came down the stairs in jeans and a green T-shirt that said Marcy School Is Purr-fect. There was a picture of a cat on the T-shirt. His younger son went to Marcy Elementary School. We talked for ten minutes. It was very ordinary. I left, unimpressed.

About a month later, someone called from the Zen newsletter staff, asking me if I would interview Roshi for the fall issue. I said yes. The morning of the interview, I woke up obsessed with the problem of what color material I should buy for curtains. This was 1978 and I had just gotten married. I drove to the Zen center to interview Roshi with that curtain obsession blazing in my mind. I planned to get the interview over with and then rush to the fabric store.

I parked in front of the Zen center and dashed out of the car. I was a few minutes late. I was halfway up the walk when I realized I'd left my notebook on the front car seat. I dashed back to the car, grabbed the notebook and ran to the back entrance of the Zen center. I flung open the door, spun around the corner and came to a dead stop: Roshi was standing in the kitchen by the sink in his black robes, watering a pink orchid. That orchid had been given to him three weeks before. Someone had brought it from Hawaii for a Buddhist wedding I had attended. It was still fully alive.

"Roshi," I said in astonishment and pointed at the orchid.

"Yes." He turned and smiled. I felt the presence of every cell in his body. "When you take care of something, it lives a long time."

That was the beginning of my true relationship with him. I learned a lot from Katagiri Roshi. I learned about my own ignorance, arrogance, stubborness, also about kindness and compassion. I didn't learn these through criticism or praise. He used neither. He was present with his life and he waited patiently for an eternity for me to become present with my life and to wake up.

Writers are not available for teaching in the way a Zen master is available. We can take a class from a writer but it is not enough. In class, we don't see how a writer organizes her day or dreams up writing ideas. We sit in class and learn what narrative is but we can't figure out how to do it. *A* does not lead to *B*. We can't make that kamikaze leap. So writing is always over there in the novels on the shelves or discussed on class blackboards and we are over here in our seats. I know many people who are aching to be writers and have no idea how to begin. There is a great gap like an open wound.

A successful lawyer in Santa Fe decided he wanted to be a writer. He quit his job and the next Monday he began a novel, cold turkey, page one. He'd never written a word before that except for law briefs. He thought he could apply his lawyer's mind to his creative writing. He couldn't. Two years later, he was still struggling. I told him, "Bruce, you have to see the world differently, move through it differently. You've entered a different path. You can't just leap into the lake of writing in a three-piece suit. You need a different outfit to swim in."

Cecil Dawkins, a fine Southern novelist, said to me in a slow drawl one afternoon after she'd read *Writing Down the Bones* when it first came out, "Why, Naa-da-lee, this book should be very successful. When you are done with it, you know the author better. That's all a reader really wants"—she nodded her head—"to know the author better. Even if it's a novel, they want to know the author."

Human isolation is terrible. We want to connect and figure out what it means to write. "How do you live? What do you think?" we ask the author. We all look for hints, stories, examples.

It is my hope that in sharing what I do, I have helped my readers along the writing path.

1

The Rules of Writing Practice

For fifteen years now, at the beginning of every writing workshop, I have repeated the rules for writing practice. So, I will repeat them again here. And I want to say why I repeat them: Because they are the bottom line, the beginning of all writing, the foundation of learning to trust your own mind. Trusting your own mind is essential for writing. Words come out of the mind.

And I believe in these rules. Perhaps I'm a little fanatical about them.

A friend, teasing me, said, "You act as if they are the rules to live by, as though they apply to everything."

I smiled. "Okay, let's try it. Do they apply to sex?"

I stuck up my thumb for rule number one. "Keep your hand moving." I nodded yes.

Index finger, rule number two. "Be specific." I let out a yelp of glee. It was working.

Finger number three. "Lose control." It was clear that sex and writing were the same thing.

Then, number four. "Don't think," I said. Yes, for sex, too, I nodded.

I proved my point. My friend and I laughed.

Go ahead, try these rules for tennis, hang gliding, driving a car, making a grilled cheese sandwich, disciplining a dog or a snake. Okay. They might not always work. They work for writing. Try them.

1. *Keep your hand moving.* When you sit down to write, whether it's for ten minutes or an hour, once you begin, don't stop. If an atom bomb drops at your feet eight minutes after you have begun and you were going to write for ten minutes, don't budge. You'll go out writing.

What is the purpose of this? Most of the time when we write, we mix up the editor and creator. Imagine your writing hand as the creator and the other hand as the editor. Now bring your two hands together and lock your fingers. This is what happens when we write. The writing hand wants to write about what she did Saturday night: "I drank whiskey straight all night and stared at a man's back across the bar. He was wearing a red T-shirt. I imagined him to have the face of Harry Belafonte. At three A.M., he finally turned my way and I spit into the ashtray when I saw him. He had the face of a wet mongrel who had lost his teeth." The writing hand is three words into writing this first sentence—"I drank whiskey . . ."—when the other hand clenches her fingers tighter and the writing hand can't budge. The editor says to the creator, "Now, that's not nice, the whiskey and stuff. Don't let people know that. I have a better idea: 'Last night, I had a nice cup of warmed milk and then went to bed at nine o'clock.' Write that. Go ahead. I'll loosen my grip so you can."

If you keep your creator hand moving, the editor can't catch up with it and lock it. It gets to write out what it wants. "Keep your hand moving" strengthens the creator and gives little space for the editor to jump in.

Keeping your hand moving is the main structure for writing practice.

2. *Lose control.* Say what you want to say. Don't worry if it's correct, polite, appropriate. Just let it rip. Allen Ginsberg was getting a master's degree from Columbia University. Back then, they were doing rhymed verse. He had a lot of practice in formal meter, and so forth. One night, he went home and said to himself that he was going to write whatever he wanted and forget about formalities. The result was "Howl." We shouldn't forget how much practice in writing he had prior to this, but it is remarkable how I can tell students, "Okay, say what you want, go for it," and their writing takes a substantial turn toward authenticity.

3. *Be specific.* Not car, but Cadillac. Not fruit, but apple. Not bird, but wren. Not a codependent, neurotic man, but Harry, who runs to open the refrigerator for his wife, thinking she wants an apple, when she is headed for the gas stove to light her cigarette. Be careful of those pop-psychology labels. Get below the label and be specific to the person.

But don't chastise yourself as you are writing, "I'm an idiot; Natalie said to be specific and like a fool I wrote 'tree.' " Just gently note that you wrote "tree," drop to a deeper level, and next to "tree" write "sycamore." Be gentle with yourself. Don't give room for the hard grip of the editor.

4. *Don't think.* We usually live in the realm of second or third thoughts, thoughts on thoughts, rather than in the realm of first thoughts, the real way we flash on something. Stay

with the first flash. Writing practice will help you contact first thoughts. Just practice and forget everything else.

Now here are some rules that don't necessarily apply to sex, though you can try to apply them to sex if you like.

5. *Don't worry about punctuation, spelling, grammar.*

6. *You are free to write the worst junk in America.* You can be more specific, if you like: the worst junk in Santa Fe; New York; Kalamazoo, Michigan; your city block; your pasture; your neighborhood restaurant; your family. Or you can get more cosmic: free to write the worst junk in the universe, galaxy, world, hemisphere, Sahara Desert.

7. *Go for the jugular.* If something scary comes up, go for it. That's where the energy is. Otherwise, you'll spend all your time writing around whatever makes you nervous. It will probably be abstract, bland writing because you're avoiding the truth. Hemingway said, "Write hard and clear about what hurts." Don't avoid it. It has all the energy. Don't worry, no one ever died of it. You might cry or laugh, but not die.

I am often asked, "Well, isn't there a time when we need to stop our hand moving? You know, to figure out what we want to say?"

It's better to figure out what you want to say in the actual act of writing. For a long time, I was very strict with myself about writing practice. I kept that hand moving no matter what. I wanted to learn to cut through to first thoughts. Sure, you can stop for a few moments, but it is a tricky business. It's good to stop if you want, look up and get a better picture of what you're writing about, but often I don't stay there. If I give myself a little gap, I'm off for an hour daydreaming. You have to learn your own rhythm, but make sure you do some focused, disciplined "keeping the hand moving" to learn about cutting through resistance.

If you learn writing practice well, it is a good foundation for all other writing.

When I was young, I played tennis. My arm wasn't very strong, and I was impatient. I was so eager to play, I held the racquet up higher on the grip than I was supposed to in order to compensate. Unfortunately, I got used to using the racquet this way. I was a fine tennis player, but no matter how much I played, there was just so far I could improve, because I never mastered one of the important basics: the proper grip on the racquet.

I use this as an example for writing practice. Grow comfortable with it in its basic form before you begin to veer off into your own manner and style. Trust it. It is as basic as drinking water.

Sometimes an interviewer asks me, "So writing practice is old hat? Have you developed something new?"

And I say, "It would be like a Zen master teaching you meditation one year and the next year saying, 'Forget compassion. Standing on our head is what's in.' "

The old essentials are still necessary. Stay with them under all circumstances. It will make you stable—something unusual for a writer.

2

Results of Kindness

*P*eople ask me over and over again how ten-minute timed writings can translate into short stories, novels, essays. Then they ask me, "But what do you do with all these timed writings?"

My first answer is, "I don't know." I mean that. What do I do after I drink a glass of water? I suppose I put down the glass and go out the door. What do I do with waking up in the morning or going to sleep at night? What can we do with the moon or a sidewalk or a garbage can?

Writing practice is simply something fundamental, like the colors black and white or moving one foot in front of the other when you walk. The problem is we don't notice that movement of one foot in front of the other. We just move our feet. Writing practice asks you to notice not only how your feet move but also how your mind moves. And not only that, it makes you *notice* your mind and begin to trust it and understand it. This is good. It is basic for writing. If you get this, the rest is none of my business. You can do what you want. You are now capable of writing a novel or a short story because you have the fundamental tools. Think of something now that you sincerely want to tell and go ahead and tell it. You'll know to keep your hand moving, to lose control and let the story take over, to be grounded in detail. Now it is your choice what you want to do.

Knowing the basics of writing practice is what kindness is about. It is about developing a foundation as a writer. Just as we would never ask a child to multiply by six-digit numbers the first day of first grade, we shouldn't ask ourselves to begin page one of the great American novel the first day after we have realized our wish to write. We have to build slowly. This is kind consideration. We acknowledge who we are in the present moment and what we need in order to continue. I often hear of a beginning writer immediately bringing his work to a critique group. His work is ripped apart and he leaves, devastated. If you know the fundamentals of writing practice and have been doing them, you have something to stand on. No one can knock you over. This is true confidence. Even if someone criticizes your work, you can go home with a trust in your experience and your mind. You can begin again and again with the simple act of keeping your hand moving, and this practice will bleed into all the other writing you are doing.

Over and over I have done timed writings beginning with "I remember," "I am looking at," "I know," "I am thinking of." Here is the last paragraph of an essay I wrote a year and a half ago in Paris.

> I look up from my notebook. There are two women across from me. They are both drinking a deep green liqueur. No, not deep green, it is emerald

green with ice. They are young, in their late twenties. The one with blond hair is wearing big circle earrings and has a dark fur coat flung over her seat. I look at their small table. There is a round silver tray with a white cup and saucer, two cubes of sugar, a white teapot with Ceylon tea brewing in it, and a small white pitcher with hot water to dilute the tea. I look at the space between the small pitcher and the teapot and my mind remembers a large boulevard in Norfolk, Nebraska. It is summer there and a man in his twenties lives in an upstairs apartment. I broke his heart. I did not mean to. It was years ago. His loving was sweet and tender and simple. I didn't believe in love then. My marriage had just broken up. I remember Kevin sitting at his kitchen table, his glasses off, wearing a yellow nylon shirt. I had a dream then that I was looking for lemon lozenges in the aisle of a drugstore. In the next aisle was Kevin and in the aisle past that was Paris. I knew about Paris and I woke up happy.

When I wrote that paragraph, I was not aware of anything but writing it. Now I see how my writing practice has affected it.

A café scene in a foreign country can be very confusing. What do you begin to write about? I started with what I saw and I kept my hand moving. It helped to steady me. I could have become frantic, but instead I applied gentleness to myself. Okay, dear, what do you know to write about? Well, I can see those two women across from me. Good, put it down. What next? There's a small table in front of me. Good, write about that.

I relied on the simple sentence structure of "I look" and "I remember," which I've used many times in my writing practice. Because I had practiced it so much, it came innately. I exercised the basic faculty of sight and let it ricochet back into memory and dream, two other things I'd become very familiar with in my writing practice.

We never graduate from first grade. Over and over, we have to go back to the beginning. We should not be ashamed of this. It is good. It's like drinking water; we don't drink a glass once and never have to drink one again. We don't finish one poem or novel and never have to write one again. Over and over, we begin. This is good. This is kindness. We don't forget our roots.

Finally, don't listen to me. What do I know? Go out there yourself into the open page. I don't want to control you. I can't anyway. I know a certain thing, I tell you about it. Beyond that, I am of no use. I can't help. All those hours of our life are our own. We have to figure out what to do with them, but having our feet on the ground is a good beginning. Writing practice can set you in the right direction, then you go off on your own journey.

Try this:

Do a timed writing for ten minutes. Begin it with "I remember" and keep going. Every time you get stuck and feel you have nothing to say, write, "I remember" again and keep going. To begin with "I remember" does not mean you have to write only about your past. Once you get going, you follow your own mind where it takes you. You can fall into one memory of your mother's teeth for ten minutes of writing or you can list lots of short memories. The memory can be something that happened five seconds ago. When you write a memory, it isn't in the past anyway. It's alive right now.

Okay, after the ten minutes, stop. Walk around your kitchen table or get a piece of leftover fish from last night's dinner to nibble on, but don't talk. Now go for another ten minutes. This time, begin with "I don't remember" and keep going. This is good. It gets to the underbelly of your mind, the blank, dark spaces of your thoughts.

Sometimes we write along one highway of "I remember," seat-belt ourselves in and drive. Using the negative, "I don't remember," allows us to make a U-turn and see how things look in the night. What are the things you don't care to remember, have repressed, but remember underneath all the same?

Now try "I'm thinking of" for ten minutes. Then, "I'm not thinking of" for ten minutes. Write, beginning with "I know," then "I don't know," for ten minutes. The list is endless: "I am, I'm not"; "I want, I don't want"; "I feel, I don't feel."

I use these for warm-ups. It stretches my mind in positive

and negative directions, in obvious and hidden places, in the conscious and the unconscious. It also is a chance to survey my mind and limber me up before I direct my thoughts to whatever I am working on.

3

Style

*P*eople ask me, "What is style? Don't I have to have a unique style?"

You already have it. We are each unique individuals with unique lives. Nobody else on earth has the same life as you, with all the same details. Even if you are a twin, one of you was born a few minutes before the other, and if you took a walk together at the age of eight and came to a tree standing in the path, one of you might have gone to the right and one to the left. Going to the left of the tree, you saw a skunk. Going to the right, your twin saw a taco stand. Style is as simple and direct as that. It requires digesting your experience, whatever that experience is, so you may write about it. It doesn't mean blanking out the skunk or being mad that you didn't see the taco stand instead. It means you see the skunk, stay with the skunk, write it down; next moment write down the next thought, next sight, smell, taste or touch.

Style requires digesting who we are. It comes from the

inside. It does not mean I write *like* Flannery O'Connor or Willa Cather, but that I have fully digested their work, and on top of this or with this I have also fully digested my life: Jewish, American, Buddhist woman in the twentieth century with a grandmother who owned a poultry market, a father who owned a bar, a mother who worked in the cosmetics department of Macy's—all the things that make me. Then what I write will be imbued with me, will have my style.

If style is a digestion of so much, it comes from the whole body, not just the head. Every cell in us exudes who we are. We know this just by looking around at people in a café. The woman in the corner smeared her dark red lipstick above her lip line. She's tapping her long fingernails on the tabletop and staring out the window. The man at the next table is nibbling the crust off his toast first, is wearing black patent-leather shoes, and has slung his briefcase on the chair opposite him.

Style in writing is not something glib—oh, yeah, she has style. It means becoming more and more present, settling deeper and deeper inside the layers of ourselves and then speaking, knowing what we write echoes all of us; all of who we are is backing our writing. That is very solid ground to stand on. Hemingway said if a writer knows something, even if he doesn't write it, it is present in his work.

This is quite beautiful. We are each a concert reverberating with our whole lives and reflecting and amplifying the world around us. This must be what is meant by the Buddhist saying that we are all interpenetrated and interconnected. But let's not get too cosmic—stay with the pastrami sandwich in front of your face, the smell of the mustard, the potato chip bags you see on a rack out of the corner of your eye.

Issa is one of the four great Japanese haiku writers of all time. In the introduction to *Inch by Inch* (Tooth of Time Books, 1985), Nanao Sakaki, who translated Issa's haiku, said, "Not gifted with genius but honestly holding his experience deep in his heart, he kept his simplicity and humanity."

That is how Issa wrote his haiku; that is how he got his style. Nothing fancy. He digested who he was: a human being with human experiences. Often in class, I read those words twice. I'll write it down again for you here. Remember it. It helps.

"Not gifted with genius but honestly holding his experience deep in his heart, he kept his simplicity and humanity."

Finally, don't worry about style. Be who you are, breathe fully, be alive, and don't forget to write.

4

Structure

*W*hen I walk into a house I see rooms. The only thing I know to do to rooms is to paint the walls white. My friend Rob, who is an interior designer, walks into a house and moves walls, raises the roof, and puts in a window where it was solid. Each time I visit his house in Albuquerque, it is a new shape. A building is his structure, but he plays with it. I see a wall as a wall, indestructible, forever. He removes the wall. That is the relationship an artist has to have with his medium.

I went with Rob to a flea market. He bought two six-foot-high abstract paintings and we brought them home. He hung them on the north wall of his living room. We stood back to look. "Just a minute," he said and disappeared. He came back with a can of whitewash and painted a thin coat across the entire canvas of both paintings. I yelled, "You can't do that!"

"Why not?" he called back over his shoulder. "They're not Rembrandts." I must admit that the paintings did look better.

The way Rob is with building design is the way we should be with the structure of our novels, poems, essays. We should use a structure but make it our own. In other words, each time we write something, we reinvent that structure to fit ourselves and what we want to say. This is not arrogance. We honor structure, but we don't become frozen by an old one. Rob couldn't take down all the walls. The roof would have fallen in on him. But if he was working on a house with a baby room, and the new owners didn't have a baby, he could reshape that room into another space.

If you want to write a novel, read a lot of novels. See what structure the writers have set up for themselves. Look at the length of chapters, who tells the story, what the writers zoom in on, what they leave out. But then you have to tell your own story. What works for you? The structure Mark Twain used to write in is not necessarily the one for you. You are alive now. You can be affirmed and learn from some of Twain's moves, but you are a different person with your own story to tell.

Structure is a tricky and important business. I tried to write *Bones* eight years before I actually wrote it. Back then, I just couldn't figure out how to set it up. I seemed to be just scattering bricks, helter-skelter. It was almost as if I couldn't figure out how to put up walls, lift the roof on the house. So I quit.

Eight years later, I flashed on the idea of short chapters, each one a separate entity. I knew what I wanted to say—I just had to find a form to say it in. Once I had the structure, all I had to do was fill it. There is a Zen saying: Put a snake in a bamboo pole. In a sense, that is what structure is. You have all this stuff you want to express—you need to pour yourself into a form.

That's what keeping the hand moving is all about in writing practice. It is a structure, a form. I want to write! I want to write! What do I do? Sit down and keep the hand moving.

Sometimes students say, "I don't know if I want to write poems or short stories." Be patient. It will evolve. What do you feel akin to? What do you like reading? It takes time to find a true form for yourself. And even then, once you find it, you have to push your edges. You can't get too comfortable. We have to work continually to keep our snake spines straight.

Try this:

Raymond Carver said in *Fires* that once he had the first sentence of a short story, he made the rest of the story as he made a poem: "one line and then the next, and the next."

Now find a sentence you like that comes from you. Don't be picky with your mind; instead, feel the sentence's integrity with your body. It can be a simple line. "I fell in love with my life one Tuesday in August." Now go ahead and lay down the next line and the next. Don't think further ahead than the next line. Don't think back. Just build that story.

Let the structure of the story unfold, one sentence after another. Place those sentences down, as if you were laying bricks. Keep each one true.

5

A Novel

After I finished *Writing Down the Bones*, I called my agent, Jonathon Lazear. "Okay, Jonathon, now I want to write my memoirs."

"You're too young to write your memoirs. Wait until you're sixty. Write a novel."

I hung up the phone. Write a novel? My friends were writing novels.

Okay, I would write one. My decision to write a novel was that dumb. Someone said, write a novel, and I responded, okay, I'll write one. Maybe that's the only way I would have gotten into it. I didn't know at the outset how hard it would be. I hear that about having children, too. That it's harder than you expected. And better, too. I had fifteen years of writing behind me, so I had a trust in myself. If I didn't know how to do it, I'd figure it out.

I was turning a corner on Don Cubero Street in Santa Fe when I thought of the hippie name for the main character,

Banana Rose. Somehow, having the name, I knew I could write the book. She would become alive for me.

And I did have a story I wanted to tell, something I'd half lived and half felt, and I needed the big space a novel afforded to tell it. But, finally, I was a writer and liked to keep my hand moving. I wanted another project. The road was out there and I wanted to ride it.

I'm sorry I don't have brilliant reasons for beginning a novel. As you go along, you make up reasons to do what you want. There's open space. Enter it.

6

Stalker and Dreamer

*M*y friend Eddie has told me something very helpful that he and his friend Holly have developed. They first learned about it from the don Juan books by Carlos Castaneda. It is about stalkers and dreamers. Four years ago, when Eddie first told me about it, it sounded dumb. Stalker-and-dreamer is a tricky issue. If it's not explained well, it can sound as superficial as "Oh, you're a Capricorn! You must be real grounded." It can be another surface way to categorize and generalize our world. I know. I once talked about stalker-and-dreamer in a writing class, and I saw people's eyes glaze over in a thin tolerance.

So it is better to start right off with an example: Eddie's two sons. Joey, the older one, is a stalker, and Matt, the younger, is a dreamer.

When Joey was ready to learn how to ride a two-wheeler, Eddie took him out to show him how he could use the curb for leverage to get on the bike, how to steer with the handlebars, how to pedal to keep going. They practiced. Joey followed the instructions, and within a short while he could ride a bike.

Two years later, it was Matt's turn to learn. Since Eddie had been so successful with Joey, he thought he would repeat the same procedure with Matthew. He brought Matthew and the bike over to the curb.

He looked down at Matt's feet. "Hey, Matt, go in and put on some sneakers. You shouldn't ride with rubber thongs."

"No, I want to wear 'em." Matt was insistent; he had his own style. Eddie gave in. Then Eddie continued to explain bike riding. Matthew half listened and then wanted to do it his own way. After a skirmish, Eddie gave up, went in the house, and left Matt to his own devices. Twenty minutes later, Eddie came out to check up on Matt. Matt was nowhere to be seen. Eddie turned the corner down the street and saw Matthew in the middle of the road, jumping up and down on his pink bike that was lying on its side in the middle of the road. He was mad at the bike for preventing him from riding it. He thought the bike was at fault. But over the next few months, Matt, in his own way, did learn to ride.

Matthew is a dreamer. Being able to ride the bike was a great victory for him, and his life was changed. He learned from the inside out. Dreamers go by an inward vision. Often they have to figure it out themselves.

Because Joey is a stalker, he was able to learn from exterior signals. Like a hunter, he watched, listened, and was attentive. Stalkers deal with the world more by perception, by looking at the outside world. Joey got his information about bike riding from Eddie's instructions, from seeing the dimensions of the bike, the road. When he began to ride, it confirmed what he understood. It gave him confidence but did not integrally change him, as it changed Matt.

American society is a stalker society. Dreamers in our society often feel like victims or develop stalker characteristics to survive.

My friend Bob and I were in Rocket Billiards in downtown Saint Paul. We were going to shoot pool. He had played a lot; I had played very little. After a few minutes, he began to explain to me how to hold the pool cue. He wasn't condescending. I knew he meant well and I actually wanted to understand what he said, but it was almost as if I became dyslexic. His words wouldn't penetrate my brain. I tried to, but I couldn't hear what he said. I thought to myself, "Here you are getting stubborn again."

Finally, I said, "Bob, let me just play. I'll figure it out by doing it." He nodded, stepped back, and sat on a tall stool. I played a whole table by myself, and I became comfortable. Every once in a while, Bob suggested an angle I should hit from and it was helpful and I appreciated it.

In the past, in situations like this, I thought I was resistant to learning new things. Now I understand that I learn differently. I am a dreamer. I have to dive in and then look up through wet eyes and ask after many tries, "Oh, you mean you do the breast stroke on your stomach? Oh, I see. I've been trying it on my back."

I tell you this because it pertains to writing. Recently I met my friend Frances for the afternoon to write. She showed me a flier advertising a writing workshop to teach plot, not only plot, but subplot and the development of character. She had just begun to write a novel.

She asked, "Do you think I should take this?"

I scrunched up my face. "Do you think you'll *learn* anything from it?"

Some people learn from outside instruction; some don't. I know people who diagram their novels before they write them or who do extensive, conscious work on their characters before they even begin. This is good. Some beautiful novels have been written this way. It is not my way. We have to come to trust our way and not think we should do it another way.

I was at a writer's conference in Bemidji, Minnesota. Several of the writers said they could never have written their novels without the help of the writers' groups they belonged to where weekly they could bring in sections to read and get comments. I thought of myself out on the mesa in Taos, thrashing away alone on *Banana Rose*. I began to say to myself, "You see what an idiot you are. You need a group!" Then I stopped myself. I realized something. "No, Nat, it is not your way." I needed to go as far as I could alone, to discover what I had in me and not be influenced too early. Instead of being helpful, suggestions too early would switch on my critic. "You see, Nat, you're doing it all wrong. Just quit." And that's what I would have done.

Ron Carlson, author of *The News of the World* (Penguin Books, 1988), who was also at the Bemidji writer's conference, said that if someone is writing a short story, he can help them, but when he hears that someone is beginning a novel, he just waves as though from a long distance off and calls out, "Good luck." There's nothing else to do. A novel is a long journey; take along any of the moves you've got for help.

7

The Quiet Place

*I*n late November I had a group of people over to my apartment in Santa Fe. We all sat around the living room, and my friend Miriam read aloud a short story entitled "Aid." After several other people read, Cecil Dawkins (author of *Charleyhorse* and *The Quiet Enemy* [Penguin Books, 1986]) walked directly over to Miriam and said, "You wrote too fast. You're scared. Slow down. You shouldn't write a short story in less than two months."

Later Miriam said to me, "It was like a guru entered the room. It was one of the most truthful things anyone ever said to me."

Miriam gave birth to a baby girl in late January. In the middle of March, I was visiting and cooing over the baby.

Suddenly I asked—I guess testing the commitment of a new mother, something I know little about—"Have you written anything lately?"

"Well, I've taken Cecil's advice and I've rewritten the story about my friend who had AIDS. I'm writing it slow, taking two months, like she suggested. Going slow is perfect for being a mother.''

"Can I see it?" I asked.

Miriam held the baby and I sat at her desk reading her new story.

Here are the beginnings of both of Miriam's pieces.

The first one, read at my house in November:

> I sat in the hospital room waiting for Fred to die so I could go to the Lexington Hotel with Larry and fuck my brains out.
>
> Fred lay in a coma, he was dying of AIDS, he smelled like a waterbed with a leak, his black skin had turned to ash, his feet and his hands were curled like claws, and he weighed less than he had at puberty. Unconscious, a pebble, a stone along the tide line, he had gathered us together. Two of his friends, both named Paul, stood over the oxygen tent sending him a warm pink healing light— as if it weren't too late for that. I couldn't actually see this light, but the two Pauls had informed me of its beneficial presence. Still, neither I nor Larry could bring ourselves to actually visualize anything. Larry was sitting and whittling away at the plantar's wart on his palm with a red Swiss army knife. Larry was six feet three, a Washington, D.C., lawyer and my ex-lover. He had slanty black eyes, and the back of his head was flat—a trait shared by the Mongols and American Indians, of which he was neither. I also knew that under his three-piece suit of summer-weight wool was a blue anchor tattoo and a BB pellet lodged by a lumbar vertebra. When

he thought they weren't listening, he whispered to
me that the two psychic Pauls were faggots.

by Miriam Sagan,
from *Short Short Stories*
(Pinchpenny, 1988)

The revision I read at her desk:

This is how Jeff died. Patrick sat in the hospital
room for almost forty-eight hours straight, watching
Jeff in a coma. A coma is neither a pleasant nor a
particularly interesting thing to watch. But when
Patrick got up to make a collect call from the
hallway phone, Jeff died. Suzanne wasn't home
anyway. Actually she was climbing the four elegant
sets of stairs to her apartment in the west Seventies.
Even Suzanne was not so rich that she felt she
could afford an elevator in that neighborhood. Her
key entered the lock just as the phone stopped
ringing. When Patrick came back to Jeff's room, a
nurse was drawing a sheet up over Jeff's face. When
the nurse saw the look on Patrick's face, she pulled
the sheet back down. Patrick stared at Jeff's face,
which had gone pure ash under the copper brown.

"Jeff died," Patrick said into the phone. He had
a roll of dimes now. Even Jeff's lawyer started to
cry when he heard the news, expected as it was.
First a remission from the pneumonia, then a second attack. When the virus finally lodged in Jeff's
brain he could use only his right side. By this time
he couldn't speak, but like a baby followed things
with his eyes: the buttons on Patrick's pale green
shirt, the arrangement of New York winter flow-

ers—purple mums, orange mums, and baby's
breath. When the seizures began in earnest the
doctors told Patrick they would induce a light coma
with sedatives.

Jeff was a doctor. The nurses stood crying at the
nurses' station because they believed a thirty-three-
year-old doctor should not die. Jeff was born
Thomas Jefferson Able, but he never told his
friends at Harvard this. It made him sound too
black, in a country way. A skinny man, he mixed
the purple ebony of West Africa with the reddish
brown of the Algonquin people.

"It's good, Miriam. It's really good." I paused. "Thank
you. I learned a lot from it."

She was pleased.

What I learned from it is that there is a quiet place in us
below our hip personality that is connected to our breath, our
words, and our death. Miriam's second piece connected to
that place, because she slowed down. In her first piece, she
was scared, so the piece was glib. We are often funny to cover
up fear, but this quiet place exists as we exist, here on the
earth. It just is. That is where the best writing comes from
and what we must connect with in order to write well. I could
take Miriam's revised second piece to Asia, to a small village
there, maybe a place that knew nothing of AIDS, and they
would understand her writing, because it came from the place
where we are not American, not gay, not a woman, not a New
Yorker.

But if we wipe out country, sex, religion—the things that
form us—where does writing style come in? Style is all these
things fully digested into our humanness, so the fact that

Miriam was brought up in New York doesn't overrun the basic emotion of sorrow.

Katagiri Roshi said in his book *Returning to Silence* (Shambhala, 1988) that it is not important whether a spiritual teacher has reached the peak or not; what is important is how he has digested the truth he has experienced and how much this truth is manifested in the teacher's life moment by moment.

This is true in writing, too. How much have I digested everything that I know and am, so when I write a sentence it comes out silent? What I mean by silent is that it communicates directly to your heart and mind, and there aren't any squeaky words that don't fit, words that are afraid. For instance, in a good vegetable soup the onion is not constantly sticking up its head for extra attention and yelling, "I'm the onion! I'm the onion!" Instead, it is contributing with the other vegetables to the good flavor of the soup. When I write about the death of my mother, that death shouldn't bolt upright like a rodeo horse and run out of the sentence. Instead, I should fully digest my mother's death and lay it silently on the page. A writer can do this with equanimity and clarity because the writer's bones, heart, and muscles have eaten it and she is willing to face her fear. So finally a writer must be willing to sit at the bottom of the pit, commit herself to stay there, and let all the wild animals approach, even call them up, then face them, write them down, and not run away.

Try this:

Take a subject, a situation, a story that is hard for you to talk about, and write about it. Write slowly, evenly, in a measured way. Don't skip over any part of it. Stay in there. It might take you several days, a week, a month to write out the whole thing. Continue to work on it every day until it is finished. Include the colors, the smells, the time of day.

Before you enter the writing each day, you might want to take a long drink of water or a walk around the block. Do something to let you sink into yourself, so you may write from that quiet place of equanimity and truth. You are safe, go ahead. Stay simple.

8

Wild Mind

I am on a backpacking trip in Frijoles Canyon, part of Bandelier National Monument in New Mexico. We followed a trail along a stream that cut through pink-and-orange cliffs. In the morning we saw deer—mule deer, I am almost certain that's what they were—first one and a little later two. When they saw us, they didn't run so much as hop away.

Now I am leaning against a boulder. The stone cools my back. Reader, even though you are not here with me, I want you to look up at the sky. Do you see it? It is a big sky. If you've never been this far west, then imagine standing beneath the sky in Ohio: a two-lane highway, the day gray, you can see the horizon all around. Nothing disturbs that view but an occasional farmhouse with a row of Russian olives as a windbreak or a white square building on the side of the road that says EAT in thin neon. The bottom line of the *E* and the left branch of the *A* are broken off.

So, either in New Mexico or Ohio, we are under a big sky.

31

That big sky is wild mind. I'm going to climb up to that sky straight over our heads and put one dot on it with a Magic Marker. See that dot? That dot is what Zen calls monkey mind or what western psychology calls part of conscious mind. We give all our attention to that one dot. So when it says we can't write, that we're no good, are failures, fools for even picking up a pen, we listen to it.

This is how it works: You've always wanted to be a writer, but instead you decide you should become a health care worker. You go to school for four years. You get a degree in social work. You are at your first day of your new job, listening to an orientation, and you realize you really did want to be a writer. You quit your job, go to the library with a notebook, and begin page one of the great American novel. You are halfway through page one when you decide it is too hard to be a writer. You want to open a café so writers can come in and sip the best *caffelatte* and write all afternoon. You open the café. You are serving *caffelatte* to all the writers in your town. It is a Tuesday. You look out at your customers and see they are writing and you are not. You want to write.

This goes on endlessly. This is monkey mind. This is how we drift. We listen and get tossed away. We put all our attention on that one dot. Meanwhile, wild mind surrounds us. Western psychology calls wild mind *the unconscious*, but I think *the unconscious* is a limiting term. If it is true that we are all interpenetrated and interconnected, then wild mind includes mountains, rivers, Cadillacs, humidity, plains, emeralds, poverty, old streets in London, snow, and moon. A river and a tree are not unconscious. They are part of wild mind. I do not consider even a dream unconscious. A dream is a being that travels from wild mind into the dot/monkey mind/conscious self to wake us up.

So our job as writers is not to diddle around our whole lives in the dot but to take one big step out of it and sink into the big sky and write from there. Let everything run through us and grab as much as we can of it with a pen and paper. Let yourself live in something that is already rightfully yours—your own wild mind.

I think what good psychotherapy does is help to bring you into wild mind, for you to learn to be comfortable there, rather than constantly grabbing a tidbit from wild mind and shoving it into the conscious mind, thereby trying to get control of it. This is what Zen, too, asks you to do: to sit down in the middle of your wild mind. This is all about a loss of control. This is what falling in love is, too: a loss of control.

Can you do this? Lose control and let wild mind take over? It is the best way to write. To live, too.

9

The Gap

*T*he mind is the writer's landscape, as a mountain scene might be the landscape of a visual artist. Just as a visual artist studies light, perspective, color, space, we write out of memory, imagination, thought, words. This is why it is good to know and study the mind, so we may become confident in its use and come to trust ourselves.

Besides understanding the way thoughts shoot willy-nilly like lightning through us from wild mind, we must understand how thoughts also drift through us from monkey mind or conscious mind. They travel discursively, fearful, blind, and dumb. What is smart is our bodies, our breath, and first thoughts coming from the bottom of the mind. Monkey mind tends to pounce on first thoughts and says, "Don't think that, don't say that," and makes first thoughts into second and third thoughts. It tries to make them acceptable, so that the urge to say "Drop dead" to someone becomes translated into

"Why, that's a lovely dress you are wearing!" It misses or covers up the real heat and energy.

Writing practice teaches us to accept, connect with and write from first thoughts. But there is a gap. Monkey mind is still busy trying to get control. A tape loop is going around in our heads, saying, "I shouldn't write this," even while we are writing.

So we come out of writing practice having no idea what we wrote, because while our hand, connected to our arm, shoulder, heart, and body was writing one thing, we were busy listening to the chatter of monkey mind. Monkey mind scrambles for territory in any way she can get it, so she tells us we're bad writers, boring, stupid, incompetent. We listen and think we wrote terribly. This is why I tell students, "You don't know what you wrote until a few weeks later when you have some distance." With that distance, conscious mind isn't so fearful of wild mind. Reading your work later is a chance for wild mind and conscious mind to meet. When the unconscious and the conscious self meet in this way, there is wholeness. There is no grasping for territory. Before that, we are traveling down two separate paths simultaneously. When the paths meet, there is acceptance, peace, nonaggression. Imagine monkey mind as a befuddled soldier who took the wrong route and arrives after the war is over. He sits down on the battlefield, trying to make sense of the raw victories and defeats.

We write and then we catch up with ourselves. Katagiri Roshi once said that we don't see that we are already Buddha right here and now. We look out and see the goodness in other people, but we don't see it in ourselves. The act of turning around and catching the goodness in ourselves is to wake up. Our consciousness, that lost, scared soldier, finally meets itself. It comes smack against wild mind and is amazed. We see who we really are. We become one whole person, not two people going in different directions.

In one writing workshop I taught in Taos, there was a man named Sun Comet. He had been a hippie in the sixties and kept his hippie name. He wrote the most astoundingly beautiful work in class-timed writings, but I noticed that when anyone commented on how good his work was, he was always shocked, as though someone just threw cold water in his face. Two months after the workshop, I heard that he was going to give a reading in a gallery in Taos. I was excited to hear him. I had a previous engagement, but I changed it in order to go.

The reading was terrible. I was so bored I almost fell asleep, as did the rest of the audience. He droned on with vague material that did not connect. It was very different from his alive writing in class. He did not think that the writing he did in class was valid. He never accepted the free writing he did in his notebooks. His conscious mind never caught up with his wild mind.

Over the years, he continued to take workshops and to write beautifully, alive, directly, and never knew it. My guess is that in the sixties he took too much LSD. The drug split wild mind and monkey mind so far apart that they could never speak to each other again. His conscious mind is still out there orbiting the planet. It never landed, so it never saw or validated the real, connected writing he was doing.

This happens all the time: People fail to recognize who they really are, ourselves included. We are slow to realize the greatness inside ourselves. Maybe we never will, but if we understand this gap, we will know how to work with it in writing. "Ahh, there we are, lagging behind ourselves again." Have compassion. If we understand this, we are not critical or afraid. We can be kind.

Well, are we ever all connected? Yes, once four years ago in a writing marathon, all of me was present with each word I put down. It felt extraordinary. Unfortunately, the marathon was with my Thursday-night writing group, fondly referred to as "the girls." They are an unruly bunch. In the middle of the marathon, they actually decided they didn't want to do it anymore and they got up and talked. I couldn't believe it. At that moment, I knew I should have stayed in the Midwest where I was living before moving to Santa Fe. In the Midwest, we would have completed the marathon. Midwesterners would have behaved.

Now, don't get me wrong. "The girls" didn't ruin my chance at enlightenment. That complete presence I felt would have snapped back after a while on its own to confusion, to engagement with the editor, but I had a sweet taste of oneness. It doesn't matter. Under all circumstances we should continue. That's why practice is so important. Just go on writing no matter what.

Try this:

Write every day for ten days in a row. Do not reread anything you have written for those ten days until two weeks later.

Then sit down in a comfortable chair and have a soft heart and read with interest and compassion what you have written. Underline sentences that stand out. Use those sentences as first lines for future writing practice. Put parentheses around sections you like. Develop those sections, if you want, not by reworking them but by reentering them with more timed writing practice.

And be brave. Let some of the good writing go. Don't worry. There'll be lots of it over time. You can't use all of it. Be generous and allow some of it to lie fallow. What a relief! We can write well and let it go. That's just as good as writing poorly and letting it go. Just let go.

10

No Writing

A student in a workshop asked, "What's the difference between writing practice and journaling? I write in a journal every morning when I wake up."

I nodded. I am often asked this. I told her that journal writing has a fascination with the self, with emotion and situation. It stops there. Writing practice lets that and everything else run through us; in writing practice, we don't attach to any of it. We are aware that the underbelly of writing is nonwriting. Journal writing seems to be about thought, about rumination and self-analysis. One of the rules of writing practice is, Don't think. We want to get below discursive thought to the place where mind—not your mind or my mind but mind itself—is original, fresh. It's not *you* thinking. Thoughts just arise impersonally from the bottom of our minds. That is the nature of mind—it creates thoughts. It creates them without our controlling them or thinking them. If you don't believe me, try to sit comfortably and still without thoughts for five minutes and just watch your breath coming in and out of your nose. I bet you can't do it. I bet thoughts arise. Writing practice knows this, knows we are not our thoughts, but lets the thoughts, visions, emotions run through us and puts them on the page. Writing is the crack through which you can crawl into a bigger world, into your wild mind. For this reason, writing practice is *a priori* to any other kind of writing you might do. And because it is unattached, you can move from writing practice right over into a short story, a novel, an essay. There are times in someone's journaling when they do touch writing practice, that disembodied, flying place, but it is not the basic nature of journaling.

The first time I heard Katagiri Roshi speak—he was fifty-one years old then, in the United States about ten years, still learning English—he said, "I have been reading your Descartes. Very interesting. 'I think; therefore, I am.' He forgot to mention the other part. I'm sure he knew; he just forgot to mention, 'I don't think; therefore, I'm not.' "

There it was! Western mind blew up in my face. Later, Katagiri also said, "I am; therefore, I think." It is the nature of a human being, like having a heartbeat and a breath. Thoughts really happen involuntarily. In biology class in high school, I learned about all the involuntary organs, but they forgot to mention—maybe they didn't know—that the brain continues to have thoughts whether we will them or not. We are not in control of thoughts arising, but behind those thoughts there is no one.

At the back of every word we write is no word. Only because no word exists is there space enough to write some word. So when we write about our feelings and perceptions, it is writing practice when we also touch the place where there are no feelings, no perceptions, there is no you, no person doing any writing. In other words you disappear, you become one with your words, not separate, and when you put your pen down, the you who was writing is gone.

This is why I do not call my notebooks journals. They are simply blank pages I fill.

11

Reading

*S*tudents who have read *Bones* come to me saying they have decided they want to write. That's good, but they don't read. If you write without ever reading other authors, you are writing in a vacuum.

Imagine a baseball player never paying attention to the other players. Mickey Mantle walks up to the plate and bats a home run. The game is over. He walks off the diamond and leaves the stadium. He doesn't shake anyone's hand or pat his teammates on the shoulder. It is ridiculous, but this is the way it is for writers who do not read other authors.

Writing is about community, even if you write alone. Some authors choose not to read anything while they are actively working on something. That is fine, but it seems obvious that the other half of writing is reading. And not just reading our own writing. That is like a snake who gets hungry and will eat only his own tail. After a while the tail is gone and he keeps going. Pretty soon he's eaten himself up.

We miss out on outside nourishment and inspiration. Read books. They are good for us.

12

Do It

I met a doctor the other night who told me he had always wanted to be a writer.

I nodded. People always tell me that. Then I paused. A doctor? There have been several doctors who have said the same thing to me. The way I was brought up, a doctor was *it*! They had money, prestige. They were helping humanity.

Then I thought to myself, "You know, I've never met a writer who wanted to be anything else. They might bitch about something they're writing or about their poverty, but they never say they want to quit. They might stop for a few months, but those who have bitten down on the true root do not abandon it, and if they do abandon it they become crazy, drunk, or suicidal."

Writing is elemental. Once you have tasted its essential life, you cannot turn from it without some deep denial and depression. It would be like turning from water. Water is in your blood. You can't go without it.

Sometimes people say to me, "I want to write, but I have five kids, a full-time job, a wife who beats me, a tremendous debt to my parents," and on and on.

I say to them, "There is no excuse. If you want to write, write. This is your life. You are responsible for it. You will not live forever. Don't wait. Make the time now, even if it is ten minutes once a week."

Try this:

Make a writing schedule for the week and stick to it. Be realistic. "Okay, this is a hard week. I'll only write twice for fifteen minutes each. Once on Wednesday morning before I go to work and once on Friday right after I leave the office. I'll stop at the Purple Plum, sip a coffee, and write."

Each week for a full month, make a schedule and see how it goes. If you need encouragement, say, "Okay, this week I'll write once for a half hour and I'll call Jamie to meet me and write with me at the Red Diner." You have to show up, because Jamie is waiting.

Even if your writing isn't completely present during these sessions, it cuts through a lot of anxiety and neuroses finally just to do it.

Try this:

Rather than daydreaming about what you'd like to write, sit down for fifteen minutes, keep your hand moving, begin with "I want to write about," and go. Stay specific and concrete. Not "I want to write about truth, democracy, honesty," but "I want to write about the time my father lied right to my face and I could taste it all through dinner. It tasted like hot gasoline."

Now, try this if you have a novel or short story or any writing you are musing about. Don't muse about it, write out your thinking. "In my novel, I want the character to be a six-foot-eight-inch lesbian with red hair. Naa, I want the main character to be a man, a five-foot-eight-inch accountant with a moustache and a missing thumb." Get in action. Work it out actively. Pen on paper. Otherwise, all your thoughts are dreams. They go nowhere. Let the story move through your hand rather than your head.

Okay. You're having a little rebellion? Go for ten minutes, "I don't want to write about . . ." Put the rebellion *in* your writing rather than rebelling *against* it. It will give your writing punch. Take control of your power.

Try this:

Use the format of "I want to write about" to explore specific areas of writing. For instance, I haven't written much about painting and visual art. Though I love to paint, it has not manifested in my writing. I'd like it to, so I did a ten-minute "I want to write about" and focused on that:

> I want to write about how red looks against yellow and how it looks different against orange, how I became friends with an ugly building in Roy, New Mexico, because I sat in front of it and drew it for a whole day. I want to write about how greedy it made me to sell a watercolor for $200 and how I painted every movie theater in the Twin Cities and each marquee advertised *Tender Mercies*. I want to write about movies, how I believe the actors are real and not actors, how I love when the movies show New Mexico so I can sit at night and watch what I see all day. I like real dumb paintings, silly ones with a sense of humor, where the artist can't really draw but tries anyway. I want to write about space and shape and I want to paint dirt roads and blue slate roads and paint the blue slate roads pink and the sky yellow and the big yellow moon on a summer's day I want to paint it blue, emerald blue, in a white sky with silver and gold stars. I want to paint pictures full of hearts and pictures with tables and dancing chairs and sugar containers and silver napkin holders. I want to say that I didn't believe in photography until I saw an Ansel Adams exhibit

in San Francisco and then I knew he walked with
mountains and the moon and then I fell in love
with black and white.

Now try other areas: politics, people you've known, animals, cars, summer, places you've never been, games, meals,
and cafés.

Even if you don't end up writing a whole book on cars,
your writing will wake up to cars, and cars will show up on the
lines in your notebook where before it seemed that people
were transported by osmosis.

What area are you numb to or do you want to avoid? Do an
"I want to write about" that area to begin to make it present
in your life and in your work.

Try this:

Okay, you sit down to make the list of things you want to write about and suddenly you can't think of one thing that interests you. That is because you are thinking on the level of discursive thought, like a water bug swimming on the surface of the water. It goes like this: "Ah, there's nothing to write about. I wonder when Jim will call. I have nothing to say." You yawn. You notice a No Smoking sign in the corner of the restaurant you're sitting in. What you have to do is drop to a deeper level, the level of your heart and breath in order to make your list and you have to keep your hand going. Here are some ways to do it.

1. Drink a full glass of water continuously and slowly without taking the glass away from your lips. Watch your breath as you drink. Watch how your mouth fills with water before it swallows. Feel your swallow. Look down through the glass. Keep drinking. Finish the whole glass. Now put down the glass, take your pen and list five to ten clear subjects to write about. Number one can be "how I swallow." Number two can be "plastic glasses." Then "my hand," "my arm," "rivers," "where I love water," "summer and ice cubes," "feeling cold on my lips." Get it? Go.

2. Take a slow walk down the block, I mean *slow* and meandering, to mimic the way you want your mind to be— dreamy—in order to drop below monkey mind. If you find yourself still obsessing about your baby-sitter, your husband, your diet, as you look in store windows, then walk slower. Feel your foot lift to step forward, feel your toes bend in your boot. Or choose a color: red. Now walk around the block and notice where red is on your walk: the stop sign, the boy's sock, the taillight on the blue Chevy. After you finish walking,

list every place you saw red. Now make your list of things you want to write about.

These two suggestions are simply tricks to get you down to a body level and out of your monkey mind. You can make up many more.

Real writing comes from the whole body. You want to get in there and live from there, not in some *idea* of your future vacation in Hawaii, while your body is driving through a blizzard on I-94 in Saint Paul. Be where you are. The best writing comes out of that.

Now, over time add other things to your list as you think of them. You should keep this list in the back of your notebook, so when you sit down to write, you can simply grab some topic and go.

But, of course, monkey mind again lifts its head when you look down your list. "Naa, I don't want to write about my grandmother's gefilte fish or her broom closet. Nope, today the Mississippi doesn't interest me or banana cream pie." I have news for you—your list will never interest you when you sit down to write. You have to cut through. Just grab a topic from your list, the first one your eye glances at, and go. Finally, no topic is perfect. You just have to shut up and write. Generating your own writing subjects is a true sign that you are becoming your own writer. We can't always write on a subject the teacher has told us to write about. Besides, you know where that leads us—back to that stiff composition about what we did on our Christmas vacation.

13

Accept Ourselves

I tell students, "Don't throw out your writing. Keep it in a notebook." High-school students especially seem to ball up sheets of paper on their desks as they write. Sometimes I stop and unball one of the papers. Bill's had a date, then his full name scrawled in the upper left-hand corner, then "I remember my mother's"—and that was it. A whole white page with blue lines wasted. I looked down at his notebook, at the page he was working on: Date and name in the upper left-hand corner, then "I remember my mother's hat." Nothing different but the word *hat*. The crumpled paper was his hesitation. My guess is if I hadn't walked by and bent low and whispered in his ear, "Keep going. You're doing fine. Don't cross out. Don't think," another sheet of paper—the one he was working on—would also be crumpled.

I say keep your writing in notebooks rather than on separate sheets of paper or in looseleaf binders because you are less likely to tear out, throw out, or lose those written pages. I say this not so much because I am concerned about the loss of a particular writing—we are all capable of lots of writing—but because it is another practice in accepting the whole mind. Keeping in one notebook the good and bad writing—no, don't even think *good* and *bad;* think instead of writing where you were present or not, present and connected to your words and thoughts—is another chance to allow all kinds of writing to exist side by side, as though your notebook were Big Mind accepting it all. When you reread a notebook and if it has all of your writing, then you have a better chance to study your mind, to observe its ups and downs, as if the notebook were a graph.

We need to learn to accept our minds. Believe me, for writing, it is all we have. It would be nice if I could have Mark Twain's mind, but I don't. Mark Twain is Mark Twain. Natalie Goldberg is Natalie Goldberg. What does Natalie Goldberg think? The truth is I'm boring some of the time. I even think about rulers, wood desks, algebra problems. I wonder why the hell my mother gave me tuna fish every day for lunch in high school. Then zoom, like a bright cardinal on a gray sky, something brilliant flashes through my mind, and for a moment I'm turned upside down. Just for a moment, then the sky is gray again for another half hour or a day or eight pages of writing in my notebook. In rereading your notebook and keeping all your writing in it, you get an opportunity to study your mind. Somehow in seeing the movement of your mind through writing, you become less attached to your thoughts, less critical of them.

We have to accept ourselves in order to write. Now none of us does that fully; few of us do it even halfway. Don't wait for one hundred percent acceptance of yourself before you write, or even eight percent acceptance. Just write. The process of writing is an activity that teaches us about acceptance.

"What did you do for your summer vacation?" That one September long ago my eighth-grade teacher asked my English class to write about this. I began with "I went." Then I thought, "Oh, Nat, can't you think of a better word than *I* to begin with and *went*! Write a better verb." I crossed out "I went." I wrote "She rode." I crossed it out. I began again. "The family visited," then "This summer," then "This past summer," then "Thinking back." Each one was crossed out. What did the first two words matter? I could have rewritten them later anyway, but I should have gotten on with it.

Next I wrote that I played softball all summer. Well, that was a lie. Not once all summer did I play softball, but I thought that was what normal kids did in the summer, so that's what I wrote. I thought it was what the teacher wanted to hear. I also managed to add, "It was fun. I had an interesting summer. It was nice."

Right off, first rule: Don't use *nice, interesting, fun* in your writing. It doesn't say anything.

The truth is, "What I did last summer" could be an interesting topic. (Uh-oh! I just used *interesting* in the last sentence after saying not to. We can also break all rules. It's good to know them, but do what you want with them. After all, who made up the rule anyway? I did in the last paragraph a moment ago as I wrote.) The problem is no one in school ever taught us how to enter a topic or gave us permission to write what really happened. "My father sat at the dinner table in his underwear, drinking beer and swatting mosquitoes, while I sat on the kitchen floor trying to put together a two-thousand-piece jigsaw puzzle of the island of Hawaii. I mostly ate Oreos. My brother had a splinter in his thumb that he got from the back screen door. No one could get it out and it became infected, swelled like an elephant. And my mother dyed her hair red and snuck out each night with a man named Charlie after my father got so drunk he couldn't see."

Write the truth. And remember what I whispered in that kid's ear at the beginning of the chapter: "Keep going. You're doing fine. Don't think. Don't cross out." Develop a "sweetheart" inside yourself who whispers in your ear to encourage you. Let's face it. You who have created the editor are also capable of creating the sweetheart, that kind coach who thinks what you do is fine. "But what I do isn't fine." Says who? the editor? Have you murdered anyone in the last day, week, month, year, decade? Probably not. Then don't worry about it. Give yourself a break. You're probably a really fine person. Call up the sweetheart and let him or her give you some compliments.

Try this:

Let's get back to the sweetheart, that person we're going to develop and give form to inside us, whose only job is positive thought. Not Pollyanna thought. Honest, positive thought.

"Nat, I'm proud of you. You wrote for three hours this morning," says the sweetheart.

"Naa, she sat at her desk for three hours. Put it all together, she wrote for an hour. She daydreamed the rest of the time." The editor or critic moves in to counteract the sweetheart.

The sweetheart retaliates. "Pay the editor no mind right now. She's a sourpuss. Believe me, if you write only one page a day, that's three hundred sixty-five pages a year. That's a novel," responds the sweetheart.

Write for ten minutes, giving the sweetheart a voice. It can be male or female. You decide. It's a mother, a grandfather, a teacher, whoever was a positive force in your life. Better yet, put them all together in the sweetheart. Throw in Superman, too, and Buddha and Harriet Tubman. Give that sweetheart power, muscle, courage, but don't make him or her belligerent, wasting time scrapping with the editor. The sweetheart has skillful means and wisdom, and knows that to fight with the editor is to get her hands stuck in tar.

But I don't believe the sweetheart when she tells me good things, you say.

Well, start practicing believing, even if you don't believe. Go ahead. Take in that compliment even if it's gonna kill you.

Why believe criticism more than positive feedback? We've been conditioned to respond to negativity. I have a friend who is startlingly beautiful. It took me a year of knowing her to realize and digest the fact that she was self-conscious about her looks and rarely felt okay-looking. In fact, she felt ugly most of the time. She was an incest survivor, and her father continually made her ashamed of her looks while she was growing up. She gave his words more validity than the flesh and blood image reflected in the mirror. Her father's words distorted reality.

This is what the editor does, too. The editor says, "You are a bad writer," and we believe her. There's no such thing as a bad writer. There is just a writer sitting at her desk practicing, putting down her thoughts and memories, visions, stories, and impressions.

Go ahead. Ten minutes. Write. The editor has already had too much power. Give the sweetheart a voice.

Try this:

Okay, let's finally put that old black dog to rest. Write about your summer vacation, that composition you wrote every fall for one hundred years. Only this time, tell the truth: What did you really do that summer? Go back to the summer before eighth grade and write about what went on. What do you remember clearly? Of the whole summer, it might be just one day when you found out that when a girl kisses she sometimes sticks her tongue in your mouth. It was old Sally. You were in the junior-high parking lot. Four P.M. under the elm tree. It knocked out the memory of every other day that summer, not to mention almost knocking out the braces on your teeth.

What did you do the summer you were forty years old, twenty-eight years old? the first summer after your divorce? the last summer before you were married?

Remember to be specific. Tell the original details. Once and for all, let it rip. Let's tell our English teachers what really went on. Believe me, as an old English teacher myself, they would probably be relieved. How many compositions for how many years can a teacher bear reading, "I had a nice summer. It was interesting. We had fun."

Okay, you lived in a small town in upstate New York and nothing happened all summer, it was boring. Write the details. My yellow cat and I must have walked to the end of the dirt drive to get the mail three hundred and eighty times in that one summer. The mailman rarely came. We checked the box eight times a day. I want to say I met Roy Rogers that summer or Gene Autry, but, no, instead I sat on the porch swing and counted the red stripes on my T-shirt over and over again.

Each day this week or each Monday when you meet your

friend at the Blue Moon to write and order those greasy French fries, write about what happened a different summer. Go for ten minutes. No, make it a half hour. You've got a lot to say. I can feel it.

14

Fresh Writing

My students often ask me, "Well, you don't use writing practice when you're writing the novel, do you?"

I nod. "Yes, I do. Writing practice gets to the freshest writing. Why wouldn't I use it?

"This is how I do it: In chapter twenty, I know Nell begins in Boulder and is driving to Nebraska. I know at the end of the chapter she has to be in the town of Norfolk. Those are my parameters: She begins in Boulder, ends in Norfolk. I say to myself, 'Okay, go for an hour,' or longer. I don't know what will happen in those miles of driving. I only find out while I write. Writing is the act of discovery. If I knew everything ahead of time, why bother writing?"

I do revisions this way, too. I leave my initial writing for a week or so, to get some distance from it before I reread it. Then when I reread it, if I see I should have said more about Nell's brown hat, I write the letter *A* and circle it where I want to add that additional material. Then on a separate page,

I put *A* at the top. I say, "Go, Nat, ten minutes on Nell's hat." I return over and over to writing practice. This continually allows me to come back to fresh writing, even in revisions. When I type it up, I'll insert *A* where it belongs.

I do all my original writing by hand. I have greater mobility: I can write on planes, with friends in cafés. Plus it feels more connected with my body; my hand moves with my arm and shoulder, which is connected to my chest and heart. All good writing comes from the body and is a physical experience.

Can you type or use your computer? Of course. It's a different physical act so a slightly different voice might come out.

15

Oral Timed Writings

*B*ob sat in on a workshop I taught in northern Minnesota. I gave the class a writing assignment of "I remember." I told them to begin with that and to go for ten minutes. Bob had to leave in the middle and he said that for the full three-hour drive back to the Twin Cities, he did an oral "I remember." He said he remembered things that he forgot existed: getting chased out of Lulu's Barbecue, going to his first wrestling match at the coliseum, his first taste of key lime pie, his uncle Dave canning pickles, the smell of the night in soul joints in Jacksonville in the sixties.

This is how he did it. It was simple. He repeated over and over again, "I remember," until an image came up, and then he went with that. Anytime he got stuck, he repeated, "I remember, I remember," until another memory came. He said the three hours flew by.

About a week later, when we drove out together to the

country in his old station wagon, he said, "Go ahead. Try it. For ten minutes. 'I remember.' Do you want a topic? Shoes."

I froze. "I can't do that. It's too naked just putting it out like that."

"C'mon."

"Okay, okay. But you have to let me be terrible." I closed my eyes and repeated, "I remember, I remember." Pretty soon, to my surprise, my mind slipped into the state it does when I write, and the memories just rolled out. I let it go wherever it wanted. I left the subject of shoes after two lines and took off to other things. At the end I landed on the countryside we were driving through, the telephone wires buzzing, the blue oat fields, the rhythm of the car, the way color disappeared in the dusk.

Then I just kept going: the Winnebago Creek on the Zen land near New Albin, Iowa; the bell I rang there; the red barn; the hot fish shop; the parking lot full of farmers' big American cars; and then us lying on our backs in gravel by the railroad tracks and throwing gray stones up to try to hit a wire twenty feet above our heads. I talked about Wisconsin and cows and wild mushrooms.

And when I was finished, there was nothing left. Not even a piece of paper with words, but I knew my mind had been on a little journey.

Later my friend Kate and I did it, sitting by the Mississippi. We gave each other topics: beds, foods I eat, cars. We began with "I remember," but that phrase was merely a warm-up. You can use "I see," "I know," or forget the preliminaries and just jump in with a stream of words.

I became excited and told Kate our next reading should be done this way. "We should have the audience throw out topics for us and we do a spontaneous oral 'I remember.'

"Look, Kate," I said to her, "we either fall on our faces,

fail completely and make fools of ourselves, or are hot geniuses writing naked poems on the breath."

I decided right then that paper and pen were passé, that giving a poetry reading from poems you'd already written and reading them off a page was contrived. I wanted to do away with everything but the voice.

I was very excited about it. Now it is two months later and I haven't done an oral writing since. I can't say why. It was terrific fun. I guess old habits like pen and paper, wanting to look over my work later, die hard. I'm not yet as good as the wind that makes its sound, is invisible, and then disappears.

Try this:

Do some oral "I remembers." Do them with friends. Do them alone.

Often students say that they had a great poem or story go through their heads while they were out running or walking or driving. Well, this is the next step. Use your mouth and articulate it, while you are out running, walking, or driving. Just let it roll. Don't think, don't be logical, don't try to control it.

This will get us prepared for when we have eaten up all the forests and there is no more paper.

16

All Over Again

*I*t was the worst blizzard in years in northern New Mexico and it hit on a January weekend. By afternoon on Saturday, the roads were closed. My friend Sorrel and I decided to walk the two miles down Canyon Road to go out to a restaurant and then see the movie *Bird* about Charlie Parker.

Sorrel was taking her first writing group on Wednesday mornings with Joan. I said to her, "Hey, let's bring our notebooks, stop halfway at the Newsstand at the Alameda Inn, and do some writing practice."

"Okay," she said.

The snow was deep and beautiful. When we got to the Newsstand we were cold. Sorrel ordered a *cafelatte* and I had a hot chocolate. We sat at a small table by the window and opened our notebooks. No one else was there but Sorrel and me and the woman behind the counter.

"Okay, let's write about sex for fifteen minutes," I said boldly.

"What about sex?" Sorrel asked.

"Anything. I don't know." I smiled. "You can start with me."

She leaned her head forward. "Well, I'm not going to read it aloud." She looked around at the small space of the coffee shop.

I threw up my right hand. "Don't worry about it. Just write."

We wrote without looking up. One man walked in during those fifteen minutes to buy a newspaper. He was wearing a red muffler. I noted it out of the corner of my eye.

"Okay, time's up. Wind down," I said.

Sorrel continued to write for three more minutes. When she looked up, she was pleased but shook her head. "I'm not reading."

"Oh, c'mon, no one's listening," I said.

"No, no, no. I can't. I won't," she said.

"I'll go first," I said, trying to ignore her resistance.

I read. I can't remember what I wrote.

Then we went into our routine again of "C'mon, no one's listening" and her shaking her head.

"Look, no one cares that much what you wrote. You can say anything. I know it's writing practice," I explained.

Finally, she read in a whisper so the woman behind the counter twelve miles away, who was talking on the phone, wouldn't happen to hear her.

When she was finished, she looked up, pleased and satisfied. "I don't know where that came from. How did I end up writing about Steve?" He was someone she'd dated five years ago. "You don't feel bad that I didn't write about you?" she asked.

"No, it's writing practice. You just followed your mind," I explained. I had forgotten how wondrous it was when you first write and discover that your mind took you to surprising places.

We continued to trudge through the snow to the Guadalupe Café for dinner. The streetlights went on. Sorrel seemed the most at peace I'd ever seen her. "It's writing practice," I thought. She accepted her mind. I'd forgotten all that, I'd been doing it for so long.

At dinner, I started my old routine. "Okay, give me ten compliments."

Usually Sorrel balks at this. Instead, that night she relaxed and was quite eloquent in her praise. After we came out of the movie theater, we walked the two miles home. It was cold and we played a word game for the first mile. We called each other affectionate names according to the things we saw as we walked. "Oh, my little tumbleweed, my sweet stop sign, my little sagebrush, my cute paved road, my little curb, my baby Wellborn Paints . . ."

Sorrel would never have done this before. The magic of writing practice had carried us through the evening and I had forgotten how good it was. I needed to be with a beginner again.

17

Not Like Therapy

*L*ast night I taught a three-hour writing workshop at Full Circle Books in Albuquerque. I called my old friend Janet, who lives in the Southwest Valley, and told her to come. In all the years I've known her, she has never seen me teach.

"Okay, but promise you won't call on me to read," she said. She was a jeweler and had never done any writing.

"I promise," I said.

During the ten-minute break, Janet came over to me. "Nat, I started to cry when I wrote. I couldn't believe it. It's like therapy. I even wanted to raise my hand to read. Wanna hear it?"

"Sure," I said. I scrunched up inside when she compared it to therapy. People do that. I didn't say anything. It's not therapy: it's the root of literature, direct connection with your mind.

Janet read to me and it was good. For the first time I saw

69

how her beautiful deco jewelry had its origin in the art deco hotels that filled the Miami Beach of her childhood.

At the end of the workshop, she came up to me again. "Nat, I couldn't stop crying when I wrote. I thought, oh, what the hell, I won't have to read, so I really let myself go. Then you said, 'Turn to the person next to you and read to them.' I almost died. But when I finished reading, she thanked me! You know, I didn't know how sad I was. My mind kept going back to all this sadness about my childhood."

I nodded. Yes, I'd forgotten that, too. That if you let go in your writing, you naturally go for the jugular over and over until you clean out unfinished business. I do it now matter-of-factly and then I wonder why writing can be so painful.

"Gee, Nat, if I did this regularly, I'd kill myself," Janet said to me.

"Yeah, now you understand. I do this all day."

Because I've done this for so long, I guess I thought everyone was wringing their brains and emotions out every day. I didn't realize that people did other things, like making earrings, bolo ties, bracelets and rings, or dancing, or balancing checkbooks. I thought we were all gnashing our teeth over the notebook.

Try this:

This summer I taught a writing workshop with Kate Green, author of *Shattered Moon* and *Night Angel* (Dell Publishing, 1986, 1989). She said something that I have to remind myself of again and again: "If you want to write, you have to be willing to be disturbed." Pretty good. It's true.

Write what disturbs you, what you fear, what you have not been willing to speak about. Go for ten, fifteen, twenty minutes. Be willing to be split open.

Try this:

An area not written about much—but which once thought of becomes a rich vein—is sleep. Try it. Write about sleep patterns, sleepless nights, sleeping in the day; how two brothers sleep together, two lovers; sleeping outside; beds you've slept in, sleeping on trips, in foreign countries; no sleep.

What is sleep, anyway? It's like the old trick of saying your name over and over until you don't know it anymore. Sleep is the other half of our life, the underbelly. We should explore it.

Another good topic, not written of much, is teeth. Go for twenty minutes. See how much you have to say about them. Don't forget your own buck teeth, your sister's braces, your dentist's bad breath, the crooked front tooth on the girl you fell in love with.

18

What I Really Want to Say

*I*n writing practice, sometimes you just go along writing, boring yourself, treading water, not really saying anything. You know it, but you don't know how to break through. A helpful technique: right in the middle of saying nothing, right in the middle of a sentence, put a dash and write, "What I really want to say is . . ." and go on writing. It allows you to drop to a deeper level or to make a one-hundred-and-eighty-degree turn in what you were writing. It's a device to help you connect with what is going on inside.

I got up and meditated this morning and then I ran. I came to the Galisteo Newsstand and had a grapefruit sparkler, then I—what I really want to say is I had a miserable dream last night. Some-

thing about Nazis and I can't remember it. Before
I went to sleep, I stuck my bubble gum on the
nightstand and I don't know how many more nights
I can go without making love. It was a blue Sunday
and I pretended I was happy watering my vegetable
garden. I'm not happy. I'm lonely. Loneliness is a
dog that has followed me for years. It's a black dog
and I have no peace.

19

Emergency Case

*I*n May I gave a day-long benefit writing workshop for the Zen center in Santa Fe. I asked Robert, a Zen priest there, to teach the meditation part and also to give a Zen lecture.

In his lecture, he said that Zen poems are marked by a feeling of space and also a tinge of sadness.

I agreed. Sadness comes from the knowledge of impermanence. Everything will eventually pass away. Why be sad? Because we love and no matter how dispassionate we become, we are not ice bricks. We are human beings with feelings.

Robert said that after he read his first Zen book many years ago—he was young, maybe seventeen; the book was *The Zen Teaching of Huang Po* by John Blofeld—he wanted to become intimate with everything. He bowed to trees and books and rows of lettuce in grocery stores. He said his friends thought he was crazy.

I thought he was wonderful. That is what Zen is about. To have an intimate connection with the world and on top of it to know about its passing. Of course there is sadness. But how sweet. And at the heart of it, what bravery. We know about impermanence, but it does not drive us into a hole. We dare in the face of it to stand up and become intimate and not just with human beings, which is hard enough, but also with the sky, water, chair, butter, cow and sidewalk. Is this not also the way of a writer?

Then Robert went on to tell something else. He said that he and his sister, Suzi, who is a dancer in New York City, discovered that they both had something in common. They both had the ability to concentrate. Suzi learned it through dance and Robert through meditation. Both had a structure to allow them to go deep.

Robert said his mother, a painter, had to create an emergency situation or a tragedy in order to concentrate. Often she threatened divorce from their father, which pushed her to an emotional edge, and with this she was able to paint another picture.

Sound familiar? We often live life as an emergency case to get some excitement, to heighten our senses. "Oh, my God, I haven't eaten since breakfast; I must eat or I'll die!" We've all heard this, might even have said it. We add drama to "I'm hungry. I think I'll have a sandwich." I know about this. Miriam says, "Natalie, I just eat lunch. When you eat lunch, it is an experience."

There are some positive ways to contact concentration. You don't have to be distraught, poverty-stricken, or miserable to be a writer. Timed writing is one way. Writing with a friend is another. It adds a healthy pressure.

Here is another way. I have just discovered it. When I have trouble being disciplined to write, I often call a friend and make a date to meet her at a restaurant so we can write together. This cuts through my procrastination.

Recently I taught in the mornings at the Taos Institute of Arts. My plan was to finish at noon and then walk over to the Garden Restaurant alone and write. Well, I found that the first two weeks I didn't write at all. At noon I began to socialize with my students.

"Hey, Natalie, want to go over to the Apple Tree for lunch? We're all going there."

"Sure," I'd say, and I'd trail off with them and the afternoon mysteriously dissolved.

If I was going to get any writing done, I knew I had to make a date to meet someone after I taught.

I called Sawnie. "Will you meet me at twelve-thirty at the Garden?"

"Well, I'm not sure I can make it," she said.

"Never mind. Don't tell me either way. I'll make believe you are meeting me and if you don't show up, I won't expect you but I'll be there."

That Monday, I tore away from the lunch crowd because I had to meet Sawnie. As soon as I got there, I began to write. Sawnie stopped by two hours later to say hi.

I said, "Listen, tomorrow I'll meet you here at one." I held up my hand. "Don't tell me whether you'll be here or not. I'll pretend you will and I'll be here."

This has worked out well. Now I call her on her answering machine. "Hey, Sawnie, meet you at two tomorrow at the Garden." I don't even have to work out time schedules. She knows it doesn't matter if she comes, but I make sure to be there because it is a date and a time and I must show up just in case.

Once I am there I have no trouble writing. The Garden is my old writing ground. That's what I do there: sit in a side booth, order a hot chocolate with a quarter cup of decaf in it, open up my notebook and go. Next week I can look at my calendar, mark down a time each day for a date with myself to write. I won't even need to call Sawnie.

This might seem silly, but it's a lot healthier than creating emergency situations in order to feel alive and get the intensity and drive we need in order to create. The sad thing is that the knowledge of impermanence is often not enough for human beings. We have to hit ourselves over the head.

20

A Reading

*I*n 1976, I spent six weeks at Naropa Institute in Boulder, Colorado, studying with Allen Ginsberg at the Jack Kerouac School of Disembodied Poetics. One night there was a big reading at a high-school gymnasium. Six hundred of us sat in bleachers. Many big-name poets performed that night, including Ginsberg, and I remember that they were all hot and we cheered them on. Then Peter Orlovsky got up. He opened his journal arbitrarily and began to read with no editing for about ten minutes.

We all know what journal writing can be like—full of our own garbage for page after page. Peter Orlovsky was no exception. He was boring; he was not entertaining us. But now, fourteen years later, his is the one reading I am impressed by. I don't remember what his journal said, but I remember my irritation and awe that he had the courage to give us an ordinary slice of his mind. He wasn't trying to be great. He accepted the unacceptable, the nothing happening, daily drudge of writing. He wasn't being "hot" and juicy. He showed us the shadow side of what it takes to get what the other readers read. I admire that.

21

Reading Aloud

*I*t is important to read aloud what you write. In writing groups, I ask people to write and then immediately afterward ask them to read it to either the large group, a smaller group, or to a person sitting next to them. It is part of the writing process, like bending down to touch your toes and then standing up again. Write, read, write, read. You become less attached to whether it is good or bad. "I wrote this; now I'll read it." No big deal. If you don't read aloud, the writing tends to fester like an infected wound in your notebook. I cannot say why, but the simple act of reading it aloud allows you to let go of it. Do not forget this. Believe me, it helps. At first it is a very scary thing to do. Your voice shakes, your heart pounds, your breath gets tight. In one class we jokingly called it the breathing disease. But no one has ever died of it, so don't worry.

My friend Geneen and I try to meet for several days every two or three months for a writing retreat. We usually write separately until one o'clock each day and then come together to read aloud chapters we have written and to talk about them. Often at one o'clock, I have come out of her back cabin in Santa Cruz feeling like I was a terrible writer, that nothing I wrote was worth anything, that I should become a plumber instead. But when we'd meet in her dining room, with Blanche, Geneen's cockeyed cat, sprawled across the table and I'd read what I had written, my mood lightened up. It didn't mean I discovered I had written something great, but it relieved that fog of doom I held around me. No big deal. And it is not that Geneen said very much. It was the act of reading aloud to another human being that did the trick.

This past weekend at the last minute Geneen couldn't get on a plane to fly to New Mexico for a writing retreat, so we both decided to do individual ones. By one o'clock on the first day, I was miserable. I knew I was not only writing a terrible book, but I was also filled with an existential sadness.

Geneen called that evening and I told her of my great sorrow. "Read me something," she said. I read her some of what I'd written and the doom lifted. Life wasn't so bad after all. I connected with myself.

Now it is the third day of our solitary writing retreat. I just heard a long message on the phone machine from Geneen. She is certain that the book she has been working on for the last two years is a terrible failure.

I smiled when I heard this. I'll call her in a little while and tell her to read me a chapter aloud. She'll feel better.

I don't know quite what this reading aloud is about, but we tend to get swampy, thick with sludge, when we write. We listen too much to monkey mind. Reading aloud gives us an airing.

22

The Cow

Twelve years ago, I was on a Greyhound bus that was heading through Nebraska on its way to Denver. I was in a window seat, munching on a cheese sandwich. It was late afternoon. On the side of the road were a big cow and a semi lying on their sides facing each other. I surmised that they had collided and both fell over. That was my logical thought. My poetry brain saw a great possibility for verse: "Oh, my God! Man against nature. The animal and the industrial." I whipped out my notebook and began to write.

Two weeks later, I was home in Taos, still diddling around with that image. I had a hundred crossed-out lines. I had an idea and I wanted to change it to a poem. My determination was digging a deep hole.

Brett walked into the room. He was the man I was living with then. "Hey, Nat, what's up?"

"Listen to this," I said. I read him several contrived renditions.

"You're still working on that cow?" he asked in disbelief. Then he paused. "Just throw it up. Have the cow riding the Greyhound with you and the semi on the road. Toss it around. Get out of that rut."

By the time Brett said that, I had already killed any initial inspiration. Even if I put the cow in the bus, got the semi to dance a jig, and me to fly overhead, I would have been pulling dead objects around for their last encore on earth. I had killed them by reworking the image so much.

If you find yourself doing this—cornering a first flash into a windowless room—just give it up. I know we've all done it. No image is that precious; just let it go. Another will come.

But the other problem was that I froze the inspiration into an idea before I even began to actually write. I leaped from the cow, the semi, and me in a Greyhound bus to logical, abstract thought about industrial life. That's thought on thought. I should have stayed with the cow, the road, the truck, the smell of Nebraska. The idea got me to pull out my notebook, but then I should have let go of everything. I should have abandoned any idea and let the writing unfold. Instead, I wanted to control it—I had this great idea, dammit!—and I was going to make it work. We become blind and stubborn.

The initial subject matter might not have anything finally to do with what we really need to say. Just keep your hand moving and let whatever is about to happen unfold. Let writing do writing. Don't manipulate it with your ideas about what you think should happen.

Try this:

It is called a cut-up. Take some old poems, journal entries, etc., and simply cut apart the lines with a scissors. Now place the lines on a clean sheet of paper, helter-skelter, mixing them up from your different sources. Throw in additional lines from the *Yellow Pages*, a dictionary, *Scientific American*. Play around with them, shifting lines, discarding some, adding others. When you have something that pleases you, glue it down on the page.

You can also do this with a friend, alternating lines from each other's work.

It's good practice. It breaks open the mind.

Now, do a ten-minute timed writing, but make the topic of each sentence different from the subject of the sentence you just wrote. At first it seems impossible, but then it becomes fun. It is good practice in making your mind nimble and willing to take leaps.

23

Animal

I am in a track club. We have been meeting for six weeks now. The instructor is wonderful and understands how to build us up slowly. At our first meeting he told us that in a year we will have the energy reserve of Olympic runners, and that if we begin well, we will run all our lives, even an hour at a time on mountain paths. And he was talking about *running*, not slow jogging!

I stood there panicked. Inside I was shaking my head and saying, "No, no, not me! Terry, you don't realize who I am. I'm just not made that way. As hard as I try, I just won't be able to get in shape."

Then I heard another voice further back in my brain. "Nat, you've always had a dream of running. Try it for five months and after that you can quit."

Yesterday morning Terry said I ran like an animal. I was exhilarated all day. I even wrote "I ran like an animal" on my sneakers, but I knew the real truth was that the week before,

I'd been on a writing retreat, sitting for hours alone in Geneen's back cabin in Santa Cruz, California. I wrote so deep into the uncontrolled darkness I didn't know if I was a word or a page or a period at the end of a sentence. I knew I wasn't a human being. I left that at the airport when Geneen picked me up and then I left it again at breakfast with her the next morning when I told her my most shameful secret. I said to her, "I'm lonely and I suffer." There we were at the bottom of my life. She nodded. We finished the rice cream, tahini, fruit, and nuts she loves to make for breakfast. Then Geneen went into her room to write and I went back to the cabin, leaving behind my human loneliness and suffering, and engaged myself with notebook, pen, and words.

This is what made me run like an animal the day after I returned from California. I didn't know who I was, so I could be anything. Terry said run and I ran. A moment before I stopped running my brain kicked in and said, "Oh, my God, I can't do this with my body. I'm gonna fall!" but I was at the finish line and I finished.

24

Home

In Joan's writing class yesterday, she said, "Okay, where is your home? Write for ten minutes."

Then we went around the room and everyone read what they had written. This is what I wrote:

> The night is my home and rain and the stars. The bell in the zendo singing me back from the wandering home of my mind and even Katagiri Roshi is my home—his voice and hands and feet and sitting there in his black robes like a crow—I'm rereading his book right now and he's a home to me, but I forgot how naïve and innocent he is. On the ride down to the airport last Wednesday I understood something about his death and I felt better ever since and I can't say what it is, but my head turned over. I can't wait to see him and I'm sorry he is suffering and I want to help. I know he

is okay and that we are all okay. That my father who walks a mile at seven A.M. to the Burger King for the free coffee they give senior citizens and then he walks back, I know he is okay and has his life and I have mine.

I ran like an animal today in track, that's what Terry said and I knew I could all along. When I fell in love with great athletes, I knew it was in me to run like an animal. I don't want to be a great athlete, I want to be an animal. I don't care about writing for itself either. I do it for something else: To dig a deep hole so I can sit and not run when the wild animals I call up come to me. I know what to do with them. I note them on the page.

I want to be like the old Zen masters whose biggest magic is having a cup of tea. I want the old boys to move over. I'm sitting with them. I'm feeling my breath, uniting my mind and body and floating on the present. They don't have a corner on it anymore. I want what they have and all along I've had it and didn't know it. Why I didn't want my father to die and Roshi to die is because it brought me closer to my death. There was no shield anymore. Just me and the death I had to dance. There wasn't anything else. I'm at home in death. Living is harder, but writing is a good home.

I was surprised that everyone else in the room stuck to a literal conception of home. They wrote about the house they lived in or a special room in that house.

Then Eddie read. He was sitting next to me, and he was the last one to read. Here is what he wrote:

I saw the old orange Datsun pickup on Agua Fria yesterday. When we bought it, they called them Datsuns, not Nissans. David Ortega was driving. He didn't recognize me in my Mazda 626 and I didn't honk. He is fat now. When I hired him, just graduated from Vo-Tech, he was thin and he ran everywhere. He was so excited about electricity, he ran to the truck for tools, ran to the shop for supplies, ran from the office when it was time to go. I don't know how he could have possibly gotten so fat. His neck was rolled over the edge of his collar and his stomach must have been hitting the bottom of the steering wheel. There were beads of sweat on his forehead.

He passed and I looked at the bent orange tailgate move away in my rearview mirror. Jim bent the tailgate when he dropped an 8-foot railroad tie on it. The back of the truck was a snake's nest of wire, galvanized outlet boxes, red Milwaukee tool boxes, an old wooden three-legged ladder, more wire—#6, #8, #14 romex—fluorescent light boxes, weatherworn and flaccid, more wire. Perched on top of the heap was the spare tire, ready to bounce off on the first bad bump. We had lost two spare tires off the orange truck that way.

Jim should keep the trucks neater, I thought. It's a sign, when your trucks are running around town looking so unshowered and unshaved, as if the business was too slovenly to ever clean up. A neat shop indicates a clear mind. Then I remembered that the old orange Datsun looked like it always had, even when it was my business. Jim was my protégé, and he was doing everything like I had. The orange truck turned left on Siler and disappeared out of sight.

When he was finished, someone across the room asked him, "Did you consider that truck home?"

It hit me as an odd question. Eddie said, "Not particularly, but when Joan said 'home,' this flashed through my mind."

I realized that most of the others in the room were beginners. They needed to loosen up. Their brains were still creaky. I understand that new students tend to be more literal, but here is a reminder to get less logical. Home does not equal 912 Dupont Street. Food does not equal mashed potatoes and meat loaf. Vehicle doesn't equal truck, Oldsmobile, Mazda. We have to break ourselves open. How do we do this? Well, the best way is writing practice, but if you're all beginners writing together, you could stay on your logical track for a hundred pages. Probably the best way is to have a wild teacher who kicks you off the ledge: "Okay, write about home and you're not allowed to write about any house or apartment you lived in, any street, town, or city. Find another home. Go!" Otherwise, what I've seen with students is they just get better and better at describing their bedroom and never leave their house. Get out of your house. Get out of your mind.

See your home as your home and understand at the same time it won't always be your home, even if you live in that house all your life. We will all die; everything changes. Write about home with this knowledge.

25

Whitman Country

Kate and I flew to New York to visit my childhood home on Long Island. Over and over I thought how generous she was to come with me. After all, all we were going to see was a green split-level in a split-level development right off Hempstead Turnpike.

When we met at La Guardia Airport and pulled onto the Long Island Expressway in our blue rented car, Kate turned to me. "Hey, Nat, while we're out there, let's go to Walt Whitman's home. Wasn't he brought up out here?"

"Oh, Kate," I waved my arm, "I don't know where that is. Probably way out there." I dismissed it.

We drove a little longer. "Well, what did you do as a kid anyway?" she asked.

"Shop," I said.

"Shop?" she repeated.

"Yup, that's it. It was my mother's remedy for everything," I explained. " 'Ma, I'm bored,' I'd cry, and she'd say, 'Don't worry, dear, we'll go to the mall.' I hated that mall. It got so bad I'd bring a book and sit in the dressing room while she looked at the racks of clothes."

"C'mon, you're exaggerating. You must have done something else," Kate stopped me.

"No, I promise. That was it. My mother couldn't think of anything else." I turned on the car radio.

It was late by the time we reached Farmingdale. I had made reservations at a new hotel on Route 110 on the edge of town. We missed the first turn to the hotel. I put on the car directional signal for the next turn. The headlights lit up a sign as I made a left.

"Hey, Kate, you're not going to believe this! That sign just said Old Walt Whitman Road."

Kate cocked her head. "Why, Nat, the Whitman Mall must be nearby."

She was joking, but I wasn't. "Kate, that *was* the name of the mall. I'm almost positive."

We asked the hotel desk clerk, "Is there a Whitman Mall near here? Where's Walt Whitman's house?"

The clerk knew all about the Walt Whitman Mall. He'd never heard of Walt Whitman. We looked up the house in the phone directory. It was a mile away.

Lying in bed that night, I said to Kate, "You know, I remember an old house across from the mall. When we'd drive past, I'd sometimes say, 'Mom, what is that?'

"She'd call from the driver's seat, 'Pleeese, *Natli*, don't aggravate me. I can't look and drive at the same time.' That was probably the house."

The next day we went to see it. We found out that Whitman often came back to visit the area after he had grown up but never actually entered that house again. The mall was built on farmland the Whitmans had owned.

Kate said, "See, Nat, your mother did know how to bring up a young poet. She did it subliminally. You shopped on Walt's land."

We climbed up Jane Hill, a favorite spot of Whitman's, supposedly the highest spot on Long Island. There was a huge boulder on top. Kate scampered up it and I followed. We could see the Atlantic Ocean above the trees way in the distance.

Across from where my mother took me to shop a great poet was born, a man who wrote in the preface to *Leaves of Grass:* "Love the earth and sun and animals,/Despise riches, give alms to everyone that asks,/Stand up for the stupid and crazy,/ Devote your income and labor to others. . . ." He told us to be free, wild, with dignity and independence "and your very flesh shall be a great poem."

Both Kate and I bought posters of his poem to bring home. Then Kate snapped a picture of me next to the sign for the Walt Whitman Mall.

That night we visited the Aero Tavern, the place my father owned for thirty years before he retired and moved to Florida. As a child, I was rarely allowed in. "It is not the proper place for young ladies." We sat at a booth and ordered two beers. I told the bartender about my father, and he remembered him.

The windowpanes of the Aero were thick and rippled. It was a brick building and the jukebox played terrific oldies, as if nothing had happened since 1962. There were Wise potato chip bags on a rack and beer mugs along a mirror behind the bar. As we played pool, leaning over the green felt, I realized I'd been looking for this bar all my life. In every small town I'd driven through, I wanted to find it. Down Main Street I heard the low sound of a train. Farmingdale even had a train station.

We met an old high-school girlfriend of mine there. Her ex-husband, she told us, had become a tramp. She saw him once hitching on the highway long after they'd been divorced.

A man came up to me. "Louie told me you're Ben's daughter. He was like an old Chevy. They don't make 'em like him anymore. I hear you write books? I just bought a Harley and I'm gonna drive across America and write a book myself."

I saw his Harley parked out front as we left that night. Kate snapped another picture of me. This time I was leaning against the dark brick doorway of the tavern. A silver parking meter gleamed in the flash of the night camera.

The next morning we knocked on the door of my family's old house. The trees we'd planted thirty-five years ago were much bigger. I could barely get my arms around their trunks.

A heavy woman in a housecoat opened the door. I said, "Hi. I'm a writer. I used to live in this house. I came here from New Mexico. I would love to see it. Would it be okay if my friend and I came in and just looked around?"

"No." She slammed the door on us.

Kate and I looked at each other. Kate said, "You and Walt Whitman. Neither of you ever entered your homes again once you left."

Try this:

Play with the idea of home. Return there either physically or in your mind and describe it. If you can actually go to visit, bring a friend who can give you a different perspective on it. For instance, if I had gone alone, I don't know if I would have connected the Walt Whitman Mall with Walt Whitman. I'd heard "Whitman Mall" so much I'd become numb to it.

The good thing about going back after many years was how different it seemed: smaller, less powerful. At the same time, I saw it from a larger perspective, as Whitman country, as a town I'd been looking for all over the Midwest for years.

If you've never left home, it is trickier. How to go home and see it new?

These are important issues for a writer. Write about the place where you were brought up. Be careful not to become sentimental. Try to be true. True to what? To original detail. To get a new perspective, try to write it from a different angle: a dog's, your mother's, a visiting aunt's.

26

Running

I met Terry, my running coach, for lunch one Tuesday at the Noon Whistle in Santa Fe. He wants to be a writer, and I want to be a runner.

I said to him, "Terry, you know everything about writing because you know running. If you go deeply in one thing, you know everything else. Just apply what you know about running to writing."

Of course, he didn't believe me. He was nervous about writing. "Yeah, I bet thousands of people come to you and want to be writers, but only a handful really are?" he asked me, wringing his hands.

I smiled. This was my running coach. I thought he was terrific, but there we had it again. The writing enigma had felled another soul. "Now, Terry, listen. You can answer the question yourself with what you know about running. Let's switch it around. I come to you. 'Terry, I want to be a runner so bad, but I know only a few can do it. I don't have it, do I?'

What would you say?" He smiled. "You'd say, 'You have two legs, don't you?' "

He nodded. "I'd say, 'Just go run up that mountain.' "

"Well, to answer your original question, I'd say, 'You have an arm, don't you? Just move it across the page,' " I told him.

"Oh, my God," Terry let out a sound of delight. "Why didn't I ever think of that before? Of course, it makes sense. Now I feel foolish. There's a hundred questions I wanted to ask about writing, but then I think of running and I have the answer."

"Yeah," I nodded.

The energy then switched and we were two peers sitting together over luncheon salads.

"Well, let me ask you this." Terry leaned in. "When I see someone run, I know everything about them, but then they want to sit down and talk about it and I can hardly say anything. Does that happen with you?" Terry asked.

I nodded. "Yes, I know a lot about someone from even a ten-minute timed writing. This knowing doesn't come from my logical and critical mind, so I too have nothing to say. It's as though my body knows where they are and what they need, but it does not stop there. I also feel the endless possibilities of the person."

Terry sees as I see. We are both dreamers. We dream into our knowledge with our whole bodies.

"Let me read you what I wrote about the time you said I ran like an animal." I opened my notebook and read to him.

"Yeah," he said after I finished reading. "Your running breakthrough came out of noplace. It seemed too early, and there was no implication beforehand of its coming."

"Well, it was my mind. After writing for a whole week, I was broken open. My mind was big. That day I forgot that I couldn't run."

"Boy, when you read to me, it went straight to my heart. Usually if someone reads to me, I have to sift it through my head and figure out what the words are saying, but your writing goes directly to my chest."

I nodded again. "Well, my writing is written out of my body, so it makes sense that it goes to your body."

"Tell me, you know when someone comes to run a few times and then quits, I feel guilty, like I just didn't get through to them. Do you feel that way?" he asked.

"I used to. Human life is big. Sometimes they come around years later. My Zen teacher said when someone leaves the Zen center, 'I can't hold them. The door is always open, but I pray for them.' "

People come and go with writing. I understand. Writing is hard, but eventually if you are serious, you have to settle and be steady, even though your individual emotions change from day to day about it.

Because of my writing practice, I understood when I joined the running club that I just had to shut up and do it even though I thought I was incapable of running. I had to just do it and not nag Terry for encouragement or criticism.

"Terry, you need to come to a writing group, meet some writers and write with them. You know, like running, we have a club and I meet Sonja, Mary, and Alice to run on weekday mornings. It helps to be with other people for support."

He smiled. "Of course, why didn't I ever think of it?"

Writing is not an enigma. It is a sport. Apply what you know of tennis, football, or swimming to your writing. I think we Americans are afraid of writing because we are afraid of the loss of control of the mind that writing entails. We are afraid of the unknown, of our own darkness. We don't need to be.

Terry said to me at lunch, "I've always wanted to write. When I read your book, I knew someday I was going to."

I nodded. "And last week after we ran, I thought this is the kind of wildness I've only felt before in writing."

Yesterday, in therapy, after having been through several weeks of hard times emotionally, I enumerated for my therapist the things I felt grateful for. It was a beautiful May day in Taos, and the sun seemed to burst out of the rocks. Outside of my therapist's window, I could see a tall yellow willow. I told her I felt thankful for it. Then I paused. "And I feel thankful for my legs."

She cocked her head to one side. "Your legs?"

"So I can run!" I said.

Try this:

Take a discipline you know well, maybe running, tea ceremony, baking, painting. Try that first and then launch into timed writings. The other skill might be able to warm you up for writing as long as it is about concentration. Concentration does not mean squeezing your brain tight, but rather relaxing it and bypassing the editor. You are so intent on what you are doing, the internal censor can't get a word in edgewise.

You can also try writing first and then launch into running or another discipline. Naturally, writing won't warm up your leg muscles and get your lungs heaving. But it might help get monkey mind out of the way with its limiting concept of the body's ability.

Runners, run first, then write.

Writers, write first, then run.

Then try the opposite. Experiment. You have nothing to lose.

27

Enlightenment

*L*ast Sunday was a beautiful day. I wanted to write but I wanted to be outside. I compromised and went to write at the Tesuque Village Market, which has outside tables along a country road. I ordered a glass of white wine and ran with my pen for at least ten pages in my notebook without looking up. Then I paused for a sip of wine. I looked up and saw four bikers sitting across from me. Two of them wore black leather vests with no shirts underneath. One had a hairy chest and was fat. Another had an anchor tattooed on his left bicep and the one sucking on a cigar had long greasy hair. All four were sitting completely still and staring at me. I nodded and gave them a half smile—what would you do if you saw four bikers staring at you? I bent my head, went back to my writing and tried to ignore them.

"Hey," yelled the one with shoulder-length hair. "Wha d'ya doin'?"

I looked up. "I'm writing."

"For school?" asked the one with the anchor tattoo.

"Nope." I continued to write. Actually, I was beginning to enjoy their attention. I realized they were impressed by my concentration and ability to keep my pen going. I felt that I had achieved the notoriety of a great athlete. After all, my agility and skill had stopped four tough bikers dead in their tracks.

"Wait a minute," the fat one said. "What are you writing about?"

"Writing and running." I looked up again. This time I gave them a big smile. Now I was the champ.

"Ridin' horses?" asked one of the leather-jacketed ones.

"No, writing. *Wri-ting*. What I'm doing now." I shook my pen in the air as though it were a javelin at the track.

"You run?" he then asked. He was not so interested in the writing.

"Yeah," I nodded. "I have to get back to it." I pointed to the page and began to write again.

When I looked up an hour later, they were gone.

That night I told Eddie what had happened. He said that I better cool it about telling everyone I'm a runner.

"Pretty soon they're going to want to run with you."

We laughed. "Yeah, and then they'll see how I huff and puff and how slow I go." Then I changed my mood. "I don't understand it. In my mind, I run like white lightning. I'm so fast. I'm the greatest runner of all time. Then when I actually do it, I'm so slow. Why is there such a big gap?

"Eddie," I said after a pause, "I want to be called Lightning Goldberg. I think it will help. The more I believe it, the more possible it will become. You know, in my mind when I run I see my legs the way they were when they were sixteen."

About twelve years ago, I took *bodhisattva* vows. A *bodhisattva* is a person who promises not to enter enlightenment until he or she has helped all sentient beings become enlightened. In other words, you let everyone else ahead of you into nirvana. At the time I took the vows, it seemed ridiculous. There were a lot of sentient beings out there. How could I possibly save them all? I was having enough trouble saving myself when I crossed a busy intersection in the Uptown area of Minneapolis. But I took the vows anyway and like pretty much everything else in Zen, I figured I would understand it much later. Now I understand it as a generous state of mind.

It is no different from saying I am a runner when I first start out and in reality I'm just a klutz in the present moment. And it is no different from saying you are a writer after you've written your first shaky paragraph and don't believe you can go on.

Go ahead, be brave, say it anyway: "I am a writer." Over time, the image in your mind and the reality will become one, if you continue to practice. After a while, you won't even notice the discrepancy, you'll be too involved in creating that second paragraph to notice writing and nonwriting. You will be engaged in the big journey. That is all that matters.

Try this:

Every morning as soon as you wake up and each night before you go to sleep, say to yourself, simply and clearly, "I am a writer." It doesn't matter if you believe it. Just plant that seed. We work in big and unfathomable ways. We work on different levels. When we actually write and lift that heavy pen to the vast page, beings seen and unseen help us. Saying "I am a writer" calls up the unseen beings. Soon what we want to be and who we are meet and we are one.

Go ahead. Say it: "I am a writer." Practice saying it when people ask you what you do. You might feel like a complete fool. That is okay. Step forward and say it anyway.

28

Junior Olympics

I flew to Tucson two weeks ago to see the Southwest region's Junior Olympics. Mary, my friend, and Matt, Eddie's eight-year-old son, flew with me. Matt had the window seat; I sat in the aisle and Mary was in the middle. As we took off in Albuquerque, there was a huge bang. I ignored the bang and was deep into reading *Love in the Time of Cholera*, by Gabriel Garcia Marquez.

Mary yanked at my sleeve. "What was that?"

"Oh, nothing." I turned to her, my eyes glazed over from reading.

"Nothing! Did you hear how loud it was?" she said, nervously.

Matt had on earphones and was listening to the Talking Heads. He didn't hear anything.

"Don't worry. Really, Mary, I won't die in the air. I've always known it."

Before the landing in Tucson, the pilot announced that a

tire had blown at takeoff in Albuquerque and we were making an emergency landing. The stewardesses showed us the posture we should take: Heads bent over our knees, hands under our thighs. They told us how to climb out the emergency exits and how to slide down the wings.

"You're kidding!" I thought to myself. "This is the way it's going to be? Right in the middle of my life—I still have to finish a book—I'm going to die!" I remembered I had two new handwritten chapters in my bag. I wanted to tear them out and stuff them in my pants. We were to leave our bags behind.

Mary had to take off her glasses. She clutched them in her hand. I whispered to her, "Put them down. Don't worry. I'll lead you out."

I became focused. This might be it. These could be my last minutes alive. My breath became powerful, and as I bent over I felt such kind tenderness for my organs—my liver, heart, lungs—I thanked them. They were about to be crushed.

We hit the runway. The sound was excruciating and went on forever, but we landed fine. I sat up. We were alive.

Eddie met us at the airport in a rented white Lincoln with red velvet interior. It was air conditioned and that is all I cared about. It was one hundred and ten degrees in Tucson. I had almost lost my life to see kids run in that temperature. It was ridiculous, and none of the kids was even mine.

The next day we sat in the grandstand holding umbrellas out against the sun. I heard Mary tell everyone about our near-death experience. At one point I turned to her. "Are you sure we were on the same plane?" She was ecstatic to be alive. I only felt kinder toward my organs.

The kids ran like lightning. All of them were magnificent, and they were propelled by only what was inside them. When I saw the same kids walking around later in the grandstand or at the hotel pool, they were just little kids with skinny long legs, but on the track they owned the world. They belonged on the earth. They were their own people and I loved watching all of them. I didn't care what state they were from or what team they were on.

I asked Matt after a relay where he ran particularly fast with boys two years older than he, "What do you think about when you run?"

He became serious. "You know, I think of nothing. I only see the track. The other runners disappear. In this race, everything turned red."

That night I sat in the cool of evening by the pool. There were palm trees and stars in the sky. I sat there dreaming: To know you belong on the earth is a good thing. To know your body is your own and not someone else's is a good thing.

What is writing's equivalent? I asked myself.

I own my own mind. I claim my thoughts. My mouth and the words I say with it are mine and no one can take that away. I can't write like Dostoyevski or Henry Miller. I write like myself.

Then I thought of a meditation retreat I went on last month. For a lot of the people there it was their first retreat and many were my age. I'd been sitting for fifteen years. My legs and back hurt, too, from meditation, but there was something I knew that they didn't know. I couldn't really say what it was and if I did say it, it wouldn't have helped anyway. What I knew was no big deal, but sitting for so long gave it to me. They just had to do it themselves.

That's the way it was, I guessed. You have to do it. You have to run or write or sit. No one can do it for you. And this book, *Wild Mind*, I am writing now? I try to tell as much as I can so I can help. It doesn't help. We have to do it. We help ourselves, and then we know something we can't give away. It dies with us. The whole thing dies with us.

Try this:

Go for ten minutes. Write what you will miss when you die. Be specific. What are things that only you know about that will die with you? "I'll miss the dew on the grass." Hey, other people know that! No, they don't. In this moment that you write it, you are the only one who feels that dew. Slow down and notice what you don't notice, and realize that when you go, you'll miss it.

Yehuda Amichai, an Israeli poet, wrote about a bank teller he used to see at the bank, how she moved to Italy to go to medical school. After I heard that poem, I thought, "You really have to be dumb to write. You have to even notice and care about a bank teller." It was a beautiful poem.

Get dumb. Don't take things for granted. When I told some New Yorkers about dumbness in a workshop two months ago, they were so relieved. They were tired of being alert and intelligent. They wanted dream time.

Walk around your neighborhood dumb for a half hour. Then go write about it—what you saw, what you'll miss. Be specific. Stay with details.

Try this:

Write everything you know about dying. Just go. Don't think, "What does she mean by that?" Dive in. We die in all kinds of ways. Who died? When did they die? how? why?

29

Lake Heron

*T*wo summers ago, at the end of August, I broke up with someone I was going out with in Taos. The morning after we broke up, I decided to go camping alone at Heron Lake. I packed up the car and left. The campgrounds were empty. I arrived in late afternoon and cooked dinner over a fire and slept under the stars. The next morning I leaned against a tall ponderosa pine with my notebook on my knees. I was going to write a chapter for my novel *Banana Rose*. It was a hard one. It was about Nell visiting her dying grandmother. I wrote two pages and jumped up. I couldn't take it. I paced barefoot back and forth on the pine needles.

"I can't do this now. I can't write this here. I need a café," I said aloud to no one. "I know, I'll get in the car and drive to Santa Fe."

Then I paused. "Nat, give me a break. Sit down and shut up and just write straight through it."

I sat down again and I wrote. I don't know how many hours

I was there, but when I looked up, the long shadow of the pine I leaned against had passed over from my right side to my left. I had written out the whole chapter and my heart was aching. I was one with Nell. I got up and went down to Lake Heron and dove in naked. I planned to swim across to the other side. In the middle of the lake, I said, "Nat, you're crazy. You could drown and there's no one around."

I treaded water for a moment. "Don't worry. We won't die in water. My father was the number-one swimmer in Brooklyn." I had a big grin on my face and I continued the crawl. I got to the other shore and climbed out. Storm clouds, big, beautiful ones, were coming from the east, and I heard distant thunder. The other side of the lake was very far away. I didn't know where I had started. I saw a tiny white dot. I prayed it was my towel, and I dove in and aimed for it.

In the middle of the lake, I stopped again. My head, like a little rubber ball, bobbed up and down in this immense lake. The water was getting rough. I looked at the sky. To the left were tall white cumulus clouds against that steel blue New Mexico sky, and to my right gray ones bringing rain were moving in fast. The sky was so big. I wasn't afraid.

The next evening I gave a reading at the Galisteo Newsstand. I got up in front of the audience and instead of reading what I had planned, I opened my notebook and read the raw chapter, unedited, that I had written the day before at Lake Heron. "A reading should have a sense of danger," my dear poet friend Jim White once said to me. I felt dangerous as I read and turned the pages of my notebook.

Try this:

Sit down with the plan to write something you have always wanted to write but have never managed to get around to. This time, though, you are not timing yourself. You are sitting down with the determination to write it through, even if it takes all afternoon or night. Relax and ease into it. Promise yourself you'll burn through, put the real stuff down, and not get in your own way. You might have a few false, nervous starts. " 'What I want to say about that time when the pancakes lay stale in their own syrup . . .' Naah, that's no good. 'I was sitting at the breakfast table with Juan . . .' Ahhh, not right." Okay, now, just go. Forget the starts, move further in. You'll fix the start later or you'll find out the true beginning is two pages into your writing. Just stay put and keep going for as long as it takes.

30

The Mink

I was sitting at my kitchen table, trying to shove words out of me for the novel I wanted to finish by June. Nothing was coming. It was like opening a vein and having dry cornflakes come out.

It was late October, still warm in New Mexico. I had on a brown sweater and I was writing about how the main character in the novel had an argument with her best friend. Boy, was it terrible writing. Whoever thought of writing a novel anyhow?

I lifted up my head from the notebook and turned it to the right. Across the room, near the fireplace, was an old round wicker chair. This time when I glanced at the chair, I saw a black mink sitting on it. She was licking her paw. She was oblivious of me. She wore a cultured pearl necklace around her neck.

I knew in an instant that she possessed all the jewels. She was the one that could make this novel work, but she sat on the opposite side of the room and she didn't care about me. She licked her other paw. I sat at the table, knowing I was nothing without her, and she had left me. I didn't know how to get her attention or how to get her back inside me.

That night I sat on the floor of a friend's house. She made me a beautiful dinner of shrimp with ginger and rice. My friend got up to get more hot water for tea. There was the mink. I saw her on the ledge over my left shoulder. She was as cold and indifferent as a stale English muffin.

I drove home. She was on the windshield for a moment. The next morning, I threw down my pen in disgust. Without the mink, I couldn't write. She had it all and she wasn't going to give it to me. I didn't even try talking to her. I knew: She had no use for me.

I called my therapist in Santa Fe and asked her if it was possible to see her. "Yes, I'd be glad to drive the hour and a half from Taos. Friday afternoon? Two o'clock. I'll be there."

It was still Wednesday. I was waiting for Friday. I gave up writing for the day and drove on the rutted dirt road into town. I stopped at Cid's and bought twelve cans of tuna fish. It wasn't even on sale. I bought it because I had to do something and Cid took my checks. I chomped into a health food peanut butter cup. I saw her above the cheeses and containers of milk, primping herself, squatting on the cold white porcelain of the refrigerator unit. I could call her up now whenever I wanted. It didn't matter. She was not going to give me anything. I was here and she was over there.

It was five o'clock. I went to Ogelvie's on the plaza and ordered a hamburger to cheer me up, to make me feel wild, because I don't normally eat them. But there was nothing wild in me. All of it was in one place—that dark mink—and as I was eating a French fry, she was on the slick Formica bar across the room. She was by the slices of lemon and a glass of maraschino cherries and she didn't care about me.

It rained hard on Friday, and the two-lane road through the gorge was slick. I wore rubber boots. I took them off at the door to my therapist's office. She had a white carpet. I sat on her white couch and told her about the mink. She cut me off, pulled over a wooden chair, put a white cushion on it and said, "Here, put the mink on this and talk to it."

"Please," I said, and the mink quickly appeared. "I need you. Come back to me. You have everything. All the jewels." I said everything I'd been saying, only this time I had a therapist to witness it for fifty dollars. No go. I was dealing in different realms. The mink didn't give a hoot about therapy. I cried. She wouldn't speak. She was over there and I was over here.

The therapist told me my time was up. "Maybe you should just sit with it until we see each other next. Try to talk to her. See who she is."

I was bent over writing my check. From over there on the tightrope edge of my perception, I heard a voice: "Quit your job." I wasn't sure if the mink said it, but at least it was something. I drove home, thinking, "I can't quit my job. It's only one day a week, teaching writing at an alternative school." It's the one thing I had scheduled; otherwise, I had all that time to face the novel. I couldn't bear it.

I turned onto the dirt road from the pavement. I drove past gray sheep, almost indistinguishable from the mesa. I knew by then that the mink had told me to quit my job. The job was in the middle of the week and kept me from going far into the valley of my writing. But I didn't want to quit. Mostly, I was afraid of what the director and the other teachers at the school would think.

I pulled up at my house and walked directly over to my

friends' house, about a quarter of a mile away. The sun was beginning to set. Michael and Ginny were a good part of the reason I built a house up there. Both of them had considerable streaks of wildness and some madness, too. Michael built solar houses out of recycled materials, mostly beer cans. At the time, he was working on a castle that consisted of four hundred tires and 150,000 cans. From far away, you could see the cans glint in the sun.

They were sitting at the kitchen table, just finishing a salad of beets, fresh from their planter in the living room. Michael got up, opened their small gas refrigerator and took out a Corona. "Want one?"

"I'll have some of yours," I said. He poured out a glass and handed it to me.

"What's up?" Ginny asked.

I told them the story of the mink. I told them maybe I should change some of the plot of the novel. I was afraid of it.

Michael, who was sitting across from me, said, "Here are two shots of whiskey." He placed two empty glasses in front of me. "This one is straight whiskey with a twist of lemon." He showed a twist of lemon with his hand. "That's your style. Here's whiskey that's been watered down. Which kind of novel do you want to write? Here." He pointed to the first glass. "You gotta write it straight whiskey. There is no other way."

Ginny, who was a Texas debutante in another life, said, "Back home, if they heard the mink story, they would call you crazy. I think the mink sounds like you—rich and dark." She rubbed my hair.

By early December, I had left my job. Then the mink and I were alone with one another. I worked on the novel every day with no teaching to interrupt me. I didn't know if the writing was good or not. I was deep into it, and the miles flew behind me as I wrote. I let the novel go wherever it wanted. I realized I had no control of it. None of the characters wanted to do what I wanted. I stepped back and let the writing unfold.

It was Christmas Eve. I went with a friend to the pueblo. It was a cold night. The cedar fires were huge to keep us warm. The Indians were bare-chested, carrying the Virgin Mary, the Bride, into the church. Sacred Taos Mountain was behind us. The sky had unleashed its stars.

I put out my hands to warm them near one of the fires. I felt the mink enter me. I looked up at the brilliant black sky and said, holding my belly with the open palms of my hands, "You are all-important. I will follow you wherever you take me and however long it takes. I'm yours. Welcome back."

31

Merging

*O*ne afternoon in February, I walked with Sorrel in an arroyo. We were arguing. I can't remember what we were arguing about. Then we were silent for a while. Then I burst out crying. Sorrel walked in silence, and I cried as we passed aspens and crossed over sand embankments.

Finally, Sorrel said, "Well, want to talk about it?" I'm sure she thought I was crying about our argument.

I said to her, "I'm ashamed to tell you what I was crying about."

"Go ahead," she said.

"I was crying because Nell just got a divorce," I blurted out. Then I started to cry all over again.

When I cried in the arroyo, I was Nell, the main character in my novel, just divorced, with the despair and emptiness one feels at the end of a marriage. Nell didn't know what to do next, but my job as the writer of the novel was to go on to subsequent chapters. I shouldn't have become lost with Nell.

My job was to help Nell, to guide her to her destiny. If I merged with her, the novel ends, both of us in a bleak divorce with no resolution.

It is good to feel connected and close to our characters, but it is also important to separate. It allows us to move on to the next chapter.

Here are some things I devised after that walk in the arroyo to break my mind from my work. As soon as I finished writing for the day, I walked up and down the streets of Santa Fe and looked in store windows, or I took a long hot bath or drank a full glass of water to signal that I was washing my work through me. Also, physical exercise right after writing was particularly good: running hard, bicycling, swimming. It brought me back into my body. Our bodies, unlike our minds, are in the present moment. In the present moment, I am not Nell and I am not getting a divorce.

But remember that transitions are hard. You're deep in your writing in another world and then you have to pick up your kids at day-care. We need to have compassion for ourselves and exercise the discipline to want to make the transition. Try not to be mad at your kids because they took you away from the novel you were working on. Really they are your friends. They are helping you leave the novel for the day. It is a matter of moving through time and bleeding through one reality and into another. It takes patience to become good at it, but it is essential. We are not our writing. Our writing is a moment moving through us.

32

Who Gave You Permission?

I met Jim White, author of *The Salt Ecstasies* (Graywolf Press, 1982), when I first moved to Minneapolis. We would have breakfast at Snyder Drugs and end up spending the whole day together, walking slowly around the city's lakes. Often we sat on benches and looked at the ducks. Mostly what we did was talk about poetry. I had finally met a person who wanted to talk about it as much as I did.

Sometimes we would recite our poems to each other. I remember the first time. I was driving Jim home and he said, "Oh, I'll recite one of my poems." And he did. A beautiful one about a deaf boy catching a Frisbee. Then I recited one of mine. I can't remember which one. He said, "Hey, that's good." And we both let out a sigh of relief. It almost didn't matter how much we liked the rest of each other's work. It was the first poem that counted the most. We could continue with our relationship.

One day after we knew each other a while—Jim was ten years older than I, a veteran poet—he turned to me. "Who gave you permission to be a poet? Was it Allen Ginsberg?" I had studied with Ginsberg the summer before. "Someone along the way has to give you permission."

"No." I shook my head. I was too shy to say, "No, Jim, it was you."

I have a friend who is widely published and is now working on her third book of nonfiction. She read me two of the chapters last week. I listened to them, my head cocked to one side. They were beautiful. "Hey, that's a novel you're writing." She smiled, very pleased. She couldn't contain herself any longer. She wanted to be a fiction writer but wasn't as sure of herself in that area. I was the only writer she knew, and whenever we got together, she said, "Let's talk about writing." Of course, I love to talk about writing and was pleased, though our friendship was multileveled and we shared many interests. I realized in a subliminal way that she was asking my permission to be a writer. Naturally, anyone can be a writer, "It's a free country," I used to scream as a kid when I was in an argument with another kid. But there's someone further along on the path, who gives you the nod, who says yes, who adores literature as much as you and so gives you permission to love this odd thing all the way and to continue with it in the face of everything.

When I say "you ask permission," I do not mean you have to go to someone higher up on the totem pole and inquire, Is it okay if I write? Write before you ask anyone. As a matter of fact, never ask anyone; always write, but it is about relationship. You know another writer and this reinforces your own love and commitment. It is not about them saying yes or no; it is about encouragement and friendship. And it is about something deep and unspoken. When I was with Jim, I quietly vowed to continue, to carry on with this great thing we both loved. I didn't stand there digging the big toe of my right foot into the dirt and say, "Gosh, Jim, well, golly, do you think even dumb old me can write?" It's more like you stand shoulder to shoulder, looking out at the vista, and the older writer points and says, "See," and you nod and smile, knowing that the vista is good and sweet and you always want it in front of you.

Cecil Dawkins was over for lunch last Tuesday. We both had finished our novels the same week. She worked on hers for eight years. Three years ago at the start of mine, I had brought her some chapters for suggestions.

I said, "You know, when I came to you, I didn't know what I was doing."

She nodded. "Yes, I know, but I figured you'd figure it out."

Last week we sat and read to each other from our manuscripts. After I read her the epilogue, she said, "Well, I think you became a writer with this book."

I was thrilled. A seasoned novelist had given me the nod. After she left, I sat on my bed, thinking, "I want to be a writer more than anything else. That's what I want to leave to future generations. If I stay true to this path, I won't be afraid to die when it's my time." I felt an invisible thread pulling me through my life. I wouldn't be so afraid to die because I would have been busy dying in each book I wrote, learning to get out of the way and letting my characters live their own lives.

But a thought just occurred to me. "Well, when do I get to live my life?"

The answer that came back to me is "You don't. Not in the old small-minded way. A bigger life happens. You extend yourself to the past and future. When you get tired of your big life, take a break. Go have a cup of tea or maybe even a chocolate chip cookie."

Try this:

Make contact with a writer you know about. If she lives in your town, perhaps call her up and tell her you would like to take her to lunch. In a small town, it might work. In a city, she'll think you're crazy. Okay. Go to a workshop this writer is teaching, meet her on her own ground but don't try to impress her—try to support her. People often tell me how much *Writing Down the Bones* has changed their lives, but they are not satisfied with this. They then want me to recognize them, and I feel barraged.

You don't even need a published author. Make contact with other writers. Go to workshops to meet people. Don't stay isolated. Make an effort to seek out people who love writing and make friends with them. It helps to confirm your writing life.

33

Time

For a long time, I wondered what the Zen concept of time was. I even heard Roshi explain it once in a lecture, but I couldn't grasp it. I remember thinking, "Oh, this is really deep."

People often ask me if my novel is autobiographical. I don't know what to say, because the deeper I got into it, the more I began to experience that my past didn't exist, that it was over and that what I wrote now about it was a new and present moment. It was as if the more I wrote, the more my past was eaten up and gone. It was like trying to turn your head fast enough to see your own face. You never can, because your face is on your face and is not separate from you. Our past is only here now. It is not in some separate moment.

There is a Zen saying: "Settle the self on the self." The past becomes settled in the present, the only place it really exists. We are only here right now. I walk into a room and sit down. Then you walk into the room and sit opposite me. I tell you I walked into the room. The only place my walking into the room exists is in my saying it. I am keeping it alive. You turn around to look and me-walking-into-the-room is gone. You can't see it.

So is my novel autobiographical? I'd have to answer no.

If I had written only short stories, I might never have gotten to this understanding of time. It took working on a novel for three and a half years. Still, only my lonely consciousness was understanding this about time. What I was seeing didn't all make sense. Where was my past, anyway? I understood when I connected with another mind in a single paragraph in *The Experience of Insight* (Shambhala, 1987), by Joseph Goldstein. Goldstein said that the only moment is the present, that we have concepts of the past and future, but they are only concepts in the mind. This must have been what Roshi was talking about, only it was so simple I couldn't get it. It was so obvious I couldn't imagine it. Only by experiencing it in working on the novel over and over did I taste its truth. *Bang!* I sat for a half hour after I read that Goldstein paragraph, facing the white wall in my bedroom without any thoughts. There was no place for my mind to go but the present. There was nothing else.

Grace Paley said, "Any story told twice is fiction." That's another way of putting the big question about time. That simple. Sometimes we don't have to delve the realms of time and space. We can just shut up and write.

34

Loneliness

*M*y great teacher, Katagiri Roshi, is sick now and I am very sad. I think about the six years I was with him in Minnesota. I want him to be well again for himself. I realize he has already given me everything. I do not need to be greedy and think I can get more from him. My job is to penetrate what I already know so that I live it day by day. So I am not separate from it.

When I finished writing *Writing Down the Bones* in Santa Fe in 1984, I went to visit Roshi in Minneapolis. I showed him the book. I said, "Roshi, I need a teacher again. The people in Santa Fe are crazy. They drift from one thing to another."

He shook his head. "Don't be so greedy. Writing is taking you very deep. Continue to write."

"But, Roshi," I said to him, "it is so lonely."

He lifted his eyebrows. "Is there anything wrong with loneliness?" he asked.

"No, I guess not," I said.

Then we talked of other things. Suddenly, I interrupted him. "But, Roshi, you have sentenced me to such loneliness. Writing is very lonely," I stressed again.

"Anything you do deeply is very lonely. There are many Zen students here, but the ones that are going deep are very lonely."

"Are you lonely?" I asked him.

"Of course," he answered. "But I do not let it toss me away. It is just loneliness."

So there you have it. There are days I think, how did I get into this writing? But here I am. And the truth is I wanted it.

35

Dreams

*T*his morning, I was in the middle of a dream. I was walking down the dark streets of Minneapolis near the Zen center. In the dream, Katagiri Roshi was sick and I was sad. I would have given anything to sit with him again.

Then the phone rang. It woke me up. It was Eddie. He wanted to say good-bye before he left for Hawaii. After we hung up, I wanted very badly to go back to the dream, to go back to those dark streets and circle the Zen center. I wanted to finish the dream. I was awake, but I went back there in my mind. I entered the zendo and bowed in front of the Buddha. To my right, I saw Roshi in his black robes. I sat down in front of a window and felt satisfied.

It is good to pay attention to our dreams. For a period of a few weeks, write them down each morning. You don't have to do anything else. Just write them down. They have their own magic and will bleed into your waking life. While you are out hoeing your garden in April, the dream you had three weeks ago of walking over the Himalayas will run down your arm. Dreams are another slice of reality, not different from where we are now—they just tell about it in a different way. They also can open up your reality. They don't have the constraints of conscious logic. I remember a friend many years ago who had taped a sign to his refrigerator: There's a dream dreaming us. If you try to think about what that means it makes your mind silly, but that silliness is good. Trungpa Rinpoche once said, "You know when your brain gets fuzzy. It feels like snow. That is not bad. It is your one chance at egolessness." So now when I feel like a dingbat and can't think straight, I don't chastise myself. I try to remember I am in an egoless state. There's a dream dreaming us.

After a big, successful writing conference I did with Kate, I felt unhappy. I couldn't understand it. I loved Kate; we were able to teach together; we got to talk about our darling writing. Everyone seemed to love it. I didn't know why I was so unhappy. Then I remembered a dream I had had one night during the conference: I had just left the monastery and I got on my bike to pedal to the city. I was going to ride to the university and I could see way in the distance all the glitz where the university was. I got lost and asked someone for directions. I didn't listen to the directions and got lost again. This time I ended up at a veteran's hospital and hung out with the retarded gardener who was working on the lawn. It was late and I slept in someone's kitchen cupboard. I never got to the university.

The dream was right. I'd rather hang out with a gardener who digs in the dirt all day. I told Kate, "Let's not do any more workshops together. We live far away from each other. I miss you. When we have time together, let's be together. I don't want to stand in front of a bunch of people and talk when we could take a walk instead."

I used dreams in my novel to tell another layer of the story or to intensify the action by creating a juxtaposition. I also used dreams to cut through the action. In one chapter Nell is camping out alone in the woods. I wanted to add another dimension to the woods scene, so I had Nell dream about her grandmother while she was there.

> By firelight, I tied a tarp to the low tree branches and rolled my sleeping bag out under the tarp. After I ate and stared into the fire for a long time, I got into my bag and let the fire die by itself. All night the wind blew hard and the tarp rippled and jerked against its ropes. I slept intermittently, once dreaming of my grandmother. She came to the woods to visit me. She had on her plaid apron and her hands were brushed with flour. She was making a cake. "Come, mamele, don't sleep in these woods. It's not nice. You should sleep in a bed."
>
> I said, "Please, Grandma, I'm okay."
>
> She shook her head. "Jewish children are never okay." She turned around and carved a heart out of the tree bark and handed it to me. "We all suffer," she said and nodded. Her face was very kind and I knew she meant no harm.

People often say to me in workshops, "But I don't remember my dreams." You can work on that. Each morning scan your mind for anything you remember of them. Even if it's just a leg hanging out the window, write it down. If you pay attention to your dreams, they will begin to speak to you.

Try this:

Have waking daydreams. Begin with "I am" and write in the present tense. Just let it roll out of you without thinking. "I am walking on the moon. Half my body is green and the other half is orange. The orange side has a story to tell, but I can't hear it. The green side is pulling me over. In front of me I see the lights of a city. I come to a river and wade through it. I can feel fish nibbling at my knees. When I get to the other side, everything is concrete and I don't want anyone to see my two colors."

It is the therapist's job to ask, "What does your green half mean? What is the orange half saying?" Your job as a writer is just to live it through your writing. Dream writing is good practice in losing control.

Now try writing the dream of a lover, a friend, someone in class with you. Begin again with "I am," but this time the "I" is another person. You enter them and dream their dream. It's fun and scary. I once did it in a writing workshop in Taos. Each student picked someone else in the class and wrote their dream. We didn't tell anyone whom we chose. Then we read the dreams aloud. I felt that I had almost gone too far into someone else's psyche.

But this is an especially good thing to do if you are writing a novel, a play, a short story. As the writer, you want to go that far into your characters' minds. You want to know them that well. I know someone who writes her characters' dreams even before she begins a novel. She may not use the dreams later, but it helps to center her in her characters.

36

Step Forward

A friend of mine wanted very much to study with Katagiri Roshi, but he lived in Minneapolis and she did not want to leave the house she had built and lived in for three years in the Berkshires. Finally she thought, "Well, I'll ask him what he thinks I should do." She wrote him a long letter telling him her predicament. Then for the next three weeks she rushed to the mailbox each day waiting for his response. After a month had passed, she realized she wasn't going to hear from him. She had to make her own decision. She sold her house and moved to Minneapolis. The day after she moved, she went to visit Roshi.

She said, "Well, here I am."

He said, "*Zazen* is at five A.M."

That's all. No praise: Good girl, you came to the Zen center. Or blame: You shouldn't have left your beautiful house. Finally, you just step forward with your life.

That's what writing is like too. Look around you. There's

135

no one there. No one cares that much whether you write or not. You just have to do it.

For a long time I thought it mattered. I thought my success in writing would finally win me love. This wasn't a conscious wish, but it was a strong one. Below that desire I found a cleaner one, a more grounded one: I wrote because I wanted to, because I wanted to step forward and speak.

It's okay to embark on writing because you think it will get you love. At least it gets you going, but it doesn't last. After a while you realize that no one cares that much. Then you find another reason: money. You can dream on that one while the bills pile up. Then you think: "Well, I'm the sensitive type. I have to express myself." Do me a favor. Don't be so sensitive. Be tough. It will get you further along when you get rejected.

Finally, you just do it because you happen to like it.

I went to Roshi last year and asked him, "Why did you say so many years ago that I should make writing my practice?" I thought there was some deep esoteric reason.

He raised his eyebrows. He thought it was a curious question. "Because you like to write. That's why."

"Oh," I nodded. Huh, that simple.

Katagiri Roshi has cancer right now and is having chemotherapy treatments. I want very badly to be near him. In the last two months I've written him letter after letter, saying "If there is anything I can do, just call." I've sent him presents; I've cried; I've wrung my hands.

Last week I called the Zen center and said that I was coming to help with anything they needed and that I understood that Roshi was very sick and I probably couldn't see him. I would just be glad to be nearby.

Now I feel aligned. I am not waiting around for anyone from above to give me the signal. We just have to step forward with our hearts and act. That's also the best place to come from as a writer.

37

Positive Effort

I woke up this morning still with a terrible cold. It was the fourth morning like this. I said, "Get up, Nat. Just get up." Instead, I lay there, staring at the ceiling for four hours. I finally rolled out of bed and dragged myself in a pink cotton dress down to the Galisteo Newsstand to write. There were lilacs and irises along the way.

Two men sitting together on an adobe wall called out as I passed, "Hey, nice day."

"Can't they see I'm miserable?" I said to myself. So what if it is a brilliant spring in Santa Fe?

During all the thick days of my divorce eight years ago, only one thing helped. I remembered Roshi saying, "Make positive effort for the good." For me it meant, "Get up and get dressed. Just get up." He meant to make human effort under all circumstances. If you make effort, beings seen and unseen will help. There are angels cheering for us when we lift up our pens, because they know we want to do it. In this torrential moment we have decided to change the energy of the world. We are going to write down what we think. Right or wrong doesn't matter. We are standing up and saying who we are. We begin with "I saw a blue horse." No one can say there is no such thing as a blue horse, because we say there is.

Go ahead. Talk about what you see: the ceiling fan above your head, the red Coca-Cola paper cup, the white plastic knife. And if this isn't enough to get you writing, knowing in this mighty moment that you create the universe, then remember me dragging my ass over to the Galisteo Newsstand to write on this supreme day when I think I'm dying of a cold.

I stop to blow my nose every ten minutes and I am sure right now I am the only one with the burden of writing. I do this not for you. I do it so I can shut up the gnawing, dim-witted critics in my brain who tell me I am nothing. Especially when I'm sick, they get pleasure out of kicking me in the teeth. "Make positive effort for the good." Even though the monsters are screaming in your face, get over there—to the desk, the couch, the café—and begin to write.

I often call myself the Horatio Alger of writing. No one ever thought I should be a writer. There were no artists in my family. There were no books in my house. Palm readers, astrologers, psychics, all said I should be an accountant. Only last year did my determination burn new lines in my palm, so that a body worker looked at my hand and said I was "a potter, something creative with your hands." I don't know why I wanted it so bad. Mr. Clemente stood up in my ninth-grade English class and read us Lawrence Ferlinghetti and Dylan Thomas as if poetry meant something. Then he switched off the lights. It was pouring outside—a Long Island rain, rain that hits sidewalks and bounces, that soaks the grass and the space between grass.

Mr. Clemente said, "Put your heads down on your desks and listen to the rain." I didn't know then that I wanted to be a writer, but I knew this was magic and I wanted more and more of it.

English majors in college show up in my writing workshops years later, after trying a career in another field, because a dream was born in them back in school when they read Dostoyevski, Thomas Mann, and Virginia Woolf, and they can't get it out of their heads. So after a few years as computer programmers, they see it doesn't give them that hard rain in the afternoon outside the window. They know there is something else and that it's in their own brain. I honor English majors. It's a dumb thing to major in. It leads nowhere. It's good to be dumb, it allows us to love something for no reason. That's the best kind of love.

38

Because

*W*atch your use of the word *because*. Writers don't need to explain things. They need to state them. "Not the why but the what." For example, I went to the store, because I needed something. I hate her, because she's a bitch. Veronica bought whole-wheat bread, because she is having a luncheon.

Because is not necessary in the above sentences. Instead: I went to the store. I needed something./I hate her. She's a bitch./Veronica bought whole-wheat bread. She is having a luncheon. You can make statement after statement. Writing is the practice of asserting yourself.

You don't have to link sentences up and make reasons for them. The juxtaposition speaks for itself. As a matter of fact, laying them down one after the other creates its own innate urgency or push to go on to the next sentence. It is a matter of grammar. Don't get bogged down in the need to explain. Just state it as it is and be fearless.

141

Try this:

Tell us what you do for everyone and not just for yourself. Go for twenty minutes. Be specific. Be brave. How are you a large person?

Quick, as soon as you finish the above writing, draw a line under it in your notebook and write from another dimension. Put in everything you *know*. Forget about what you *do*. Go for twenty minutes. Make use of everything. Don't be logical. Let it rip.

39

Very and Really

*B*e careful of the use of the word *very*. Usually we don't need it. It's a word that emphasizes something that has already been stated. "The boy was *very* timid." It doesn't add that much; and, as a matter of fact, "The boy was timid" gives us a more direct statement. We hear *timid* better without the hoopla of *very*. *Very* lessens the presence of the word it is modifying. "It is very good." Take out *very*. "It is good." This is a brave statement and is rarely used. Simple, direct, to the point. No doilies of lacy *verys* are put around the quality of good. Just *good*. "He was very dead"—let's be honest. Someone's either dead or they're not. There is a clear line between life and death. Let's draw that line. Be aware of *very* and how you use it.

It is the same with the word *really*. "It was *really* fine." It almost sounds as though the writer doesn't believe it was fine—"Really, I promise, it was fine." "It was fine" is a simple, direct statement that you can stand behind. We don't have to fluff it up. Words and sentence structure reflect the integrity of a writer. State clearly what you have to say. Don't be afraid. Step forward.

I find when I speak I use *really* a lot, because underneath I don't trust people's attention. I am trying to get them to "really" listen. Someone is either listening or not. We don't have to get them to "really" do it.

We can just settle back into our bodies and write, neither hiding nor reaching out. Just being present. Then we write out of true emptiness. We write because we write and for no other reason. That is good.

Try this:

At Eddie's men's group last week, he told me that they had a discussion on spirituality. Eddie said it was kind of vague and too long.

I said they should have gone around the room and let each person tell about a spiritual experience he'd had.

Do that now, whether you are a man or a woman. Write about a time you felt at one with God or the Goddess, whatever. Tell the details. Share the experience. Begin, if you want, with the mundane: "I was dusting the cabinet, when I saw the dust on the mirror form into a huge cross . . ." or "I was frying a tortilla when I saw Christ's face in it. I quickly pulled it out of the oil and built an altar. I put stones, twigs, sage, some parsley on the altar . . ." Take your time in the telling. We've all had spiritual experiences of some sort. Write them now and legitimize them.

40

The Dead Year

*I*t has been a long time since I first began to write, so as hard as I try to remember, it is difficult sometimes to get back to beginner's mind. But running track has brought back the memory of beginning clearly and that is good. It gives me more compassion for my writing students. I run up a hill and I have seven more to go and all I hear in my head, like a chant, for the first fifteen minutes is "I can't, I can't, I can't," and my body is a dead weight that I manage to move at the pace of the erosion of the Egyptian pyramids.

And so I remember the first dead year of writing, when I wanted to be a writer so bad. I was twenty-four years old and I didn't know how. I didn't know how writers got their ideas or what they wrote about. I'd sit at a kitchen table, trying to think of something to write. "Let's see," I'd say to myself. I'd look around the room. "The ceiling is white," I'd write in my notebook. Then I'd sit for another ten minutes. I'd conjure up another line: "My knee hurts." Then I'd get a little inspiration. "I had a dream last night, but I forgot it." This was hard, painful, but good. I was creating my own relationship with writing. Over time, in facing this dead sludge, I claimed writing as my own.

Writing communally, in groups, with a friend at a café, is good encouragement, but the underbelly of writing is facing that inertia, sitting in it, staying in it and not running away. This gives you a dead-center power. Even if your friend forgets your writing date, you will write. Even if your family criticizes you, you are broke, you think you're stupid, you have arthritis, you will write.

I'm thinking of a woman I know in Boulder, Colorado. She came to me, I thought, for a one-hour writing session to go over her work. She flew down from Denver. She walked in my kitchen, sat down at my kitchen table, and broke down crying. "I want to be a writer. I own an ad agency. I'm very successful, but I want to be a writer."

"So be a writer. Sell the agency." I'm not good as a therapist. I tell them what to do.

She nodded.

I thought, "This is what has become of my life. I want to go write and here I sit counseling strangers."

To my surprise she came to my summer workshop three months later. Her business was in the process of being sold. I thought, "Gee, she's serious."

In the winter, on my way to Minnesota, I had to change planes in Denver. I had an hour layover. I called Daniella on the phone. It was a toll-free call. "Hi, how you doing?" It was late morning.

"Natalie, oh, my God! I've been sitting here, trying to write all morning. I have my desk in front of the window, clean paper, a pen. Now what do I do?"

I told her to get her hand moving.

I wanted to tell her that this first year isn't a bucking bronco—there's little excitement. It's more like walking through thick desert heat with no end in sight. You look for an image and it becomes a mirage. Everything is empty. Nothing you write holds. It's like trying to grab a fistful of sand with an open hand—the granules run through your spread fingers. You can say it's a great test. "Uh, oh. Did I make a mistake? Should I have kept my well-paying job? My parents think I'm wasting my life; the kids want to know what I do all day." Things outside ourselves will always beg us to conform, but they aren't the real challenge. They are just an excuse or an out when we can't face that inertia inside us, that resistance and boredom that arise as soon as we make an effort toward something we deeply want.

That dead feeling hits hard and permeates the first year. It comes back to test you often in the following years, but if you get through the first year, then you know about it. It will never have the power to defeat you again.

I often say to myself now when writing is hard, "There is no such thing as failure." The only failure in writing is when you stop doing it. Then you fail yourself. You affirm your resistance. Don't do that. Let the outside world scream at you. Create an inner world of determination. When someone complained about getting up at five A.M. for sitting meditation, Katagiri Roshi said, "Make positive effort for the good." I repeat that often to myself when pushing the pen across the page feels like I, alone, have the responsibility to make the earth turn around the sun. Well, it's probably true. Each of us does create the world. We'd better get to work.

I saw Daniella a week ago at a workshop. She had gotten through the trial year. I could feel her determination. This doesn't mean it was all clear to her, but another person watching her could tell.

Often after getting through that dead year, people go back to work and earn a living. It sounds like they gave up on writing, but, no, they proved something to themselves. They won't abandon writing now, even if they have to pay the mortgage, go to PTA meetings, do grocery shopping. It's theirs. They've claimed it. There is a personal power in that. No one can take it away.

41

Another Arm Moving

I'm back again at the restaurant on the plaza in Taos, sitting next to Adair. We meet three mornings a week and she is a strict believer in my own motto, Shut up and write.

Whenever I want to socialize, she says, "Okay, go for two hours."

I say, "You're kidding. C'mon," but by the time I say, "C'mon," she is already deep into her writing, so I have to begin with my own. I go into *Banana Rose*.

In one chapter I was working on, Nell was going to find out that her boyfriend was sleeping around, but I knew I just couldn't dive into that fact. I had to sidle into it slowly. Otherwise, I could have reduced the novel to stick figures doing human acts: chapter 1, Nell loves Gauguin; chapter 2, Gauguin kisses someone else; chapter 3, Nell faints. I had to slow things down, give the weather, the clothes, Nell's face. A novel doesn't move zip-zip. You have to keep the reader's attention. The best way to do this is to enter the life of the characters.

I tell my students you can't plant a grass seed and then stick your finger in the seed and yank out a blade of grass. It doesn't work like that. We have to be patient to let the blade of grass grow. It takes many elements: sun, cloud, earth, insects, seed. This is true in writing, too. A lot led up to Nell's boyfriend sleeping with someone else. And even in the chapter I was just about to write, it took time for it to hit Nell.

I tugged at Adair's sleeve. She was writing furiously and I didn't know how to begin.

"Adair, what are you writing about?" I asked.

"1978, what happened to me then," she said quickly, not stopping pen on paper.

I drifted off. 1978? What did I do then? *Shogun*! I read *Shogun*. I began to write: Nell was on her porch swing reading *Shogun*. From there I moved into the heart of the matter. I made it summer, because it was summer that day in Taos when I wrote. I let the weather in the present inform me.

It is good to take cues from the present. It makes the writing lively. Another time I wrote about Nell's divorce. I glanced up. I saw a box of Constant Comment tea bags on the ledge over the door of the restaurant. Sure enough, the chapter opened with Nell drinking Constant Comment at a café in Minneapolis. But the divorce in the novel was chronologically in the fall so I had to make it October in that chapter, even though it was snowing out in Taos the day I wrote it. Sometimes I could let the present inform the novel and sometimes I couldn't.

A novel makes you behave. There are constrictions. I think of poetry as the final freedom. Each poem is its own universe, but it, too, is a hard freedom. There is no career in poetry and though you might practice, you also have to wait patiently for a true poem to come. Poetry is about the divine; a novel is about work and learning to behave. That was not easy for me. The novel was good practice.

Sometimes Adair could only stay an hour or two, and after she left, I stayed on, a solitary writer writing in a race against only her own best time. I would go far into Nell's life and leave my own. I'd order toast in the restaurant. Then juice. Anything to keep my table. I learned the waitresses' names. At noon, I'd leave and go out for lunch to another place and sometimes come back to "my" restaurant at about two to continue writing.

Writing is a democratic act. There is no hierarchy. So what if you are the recipient of the Nobel Prize in literature? You have to wake up the next day and start another story. It didn't matter that Adair had just begun to do writing practice and I had done it for fifteen years. Actually, she brought a freshness to it. All we need is another arm moving across a page. Don't be snooty, thinking you need to write with someone great. Who's great? Just get another body and get going.

42

Wanting It Bad

I didn't know anything as a kid. I liked Oreo cookies, my grandmother's chopped liver. Besides that, I was asleep in a split-level development on Long Island among Italians and Irish Catholics who had altars where our linen closet was.

Then, when I was twelve, I learned tennis in summer camp. I didn't actually learn it. I stepped on the court and was whole. If I had to learn it, I probably would have quit. That's what kind of kid I was—I had no perseverance—but tennis I knew. It was a song and I played it. Day after day. All day. I skipped softball, volleyball, swimming, canoeing, dramatics, arts and crafts. I played with eight-year-olds, twelve-year-olds, sixteen-year-olds, anyone who came along. I lived on the court and whoever I played entered my domain. I was happy to rally, but if we played games, I won. But mind you, I didn't care about winning or losing. I was outside those realms. I lusted for the sound of that fuzzy ball hitting the center of my racquet, the stretch of my young arm, the soles

153

of my sneakers rubbed to swirls. I was never tired or hot or sweaty. I was a god. I stepped out of the realm of thought.

This was the first time I loved something all for myself. It was mine. I didn't know this then. I just went to the courts with my sixteen-dollar wooden Slazenger tennis racquet every day.

When I was fourteen, Bruce Berkowitz, who was a camp waiter and sixteen, went home to Brooklyn at the end of August, declaring he would beat me the next summer. He practiced all winter, and when we met again at the camp bus in the Howard Johnson's parking lot in Westchester, he had three racquets in his duffel bag. He challenged me for a game the day after we arrived at camp up in the Adirondacks.

I walked on the court like a prince, not like a princess. Princesses are delicate. They can feel peas under twelve mattresses when they lie down to sleep. I was a prince in the land I owned: the tennis court. I wasn't arrogant. I knew who I was: no one. Just an eye and a hand, a body to hold a racquet and, most important, I couldn't have cared less whether Bruce Berkowitz beat me or not.

Of course, this attitude totally discombobulated Bruce. He fell apart. I beat him 6–0. I'm sure he did become very good over the winter, probably better than I was, especially since I never played tennis at home on Long Island. When I went home, I went back to eating Oreo cookies and watching television.

It had to do with the mind. I didn't have a mind when I played. Bruce did. He had expectations, goals, desires. When the tennis ball was coming at him, he was thinking where he could place it to win a point. I wasn't thinking anything. It was the only place I was free. It was a gift. Now, much older, I know that I would have had to work at it to keep being free. I would have had to practice and refine my moves. Instead, the summer I turned sixteen I had a boyfriend and never stepped on the court.

That is how writing was for me, too, when I wrote my first poem at twenty-three years of age. I felt whole and complete in myself. But, unlike tennis, with writing I continued and have come up against some miserable times when I've wanted to quit. I continued then, too. It's a process. I didn't marry writing all at once, but over time as I stayed connected to it under all circumstances, it has strenthened my resolve. Now, whether I like it or not, publish or not, it is the ground I walk on, my basic practice. And in keeping this commitment, it has taken me deep and has rooted me.

I was surprised when I first moved to Santa Fe and taught writing workshops where people came with the idea that this writing might save them. Last month they tried rolfing and this month it was writing. It is good to try different things, but eventually we must settle on one thing and commit ourselves. Otherwise we are always drifting and there is no peace. To stay with one thing gives us an opportunity to penetrate our lives and be free.

Clarity and perseverance are difficult in American society because the basis of capitalism is greed and dissatisfaction. There is always a better stereo system, television, car, and shoe. Why should we settle on writing, when next week we can take up hang gliding? The American economic system feeds monkey mind. We stimulate monkey mind when we swing from one preoccupation to the next.

Often I have students who want to become writers and to make a lot of money writing to replace the comfortable, but unsatisfactory, job they have now. I tell them, "You have to be willing to be uncomfortable and poor, maybe for the rest of your life. You have to have a big vision and enter the *sangha* [spiritual community] of writers all over the world, past, present and future, for eons. So keep your well-paying job while you test out your commitment."

Hemingway writes in *Green Hills of Africa* about young American men who went to Paris for two years to try out being artists. If they weren't successful, they planned to go home and work in their fathers' businesses. Hemingway said that that is the wrong attitude, that you have to be willing to give it as long as it takes.

You have to let writing eat your life and follow it where it takes you. You fit into it; it doesn't fit neatly into your life. It makes you wild. Kate said that she would put Raphael, her first son, to bed at about nine and then write until midnight or one. (She also had a poet-in-the-schools job during the day.) She said to the outside world she looked normal—changing diapers, making food—but inside she was wild. How could she work all day, have a baby and write? She wanted it bad; that's finally what moves you, not how it will conveniently fit in with the rest of your life.

Let yourself burn, let yourself want something bad. It's a life force. When I first started writing at twenty-three, I thought it was a lust more than a passion. I remember hitchhiking to Chicago—I was living in Ann Arbor then—with a friend and her dog named Lakota. We were going to visit her aunt. I saw a poster advertising a poetry contest to be held in a warehouse. Fifty poets had three minutes each to read in front of four judges. It was happening the next day, a Saturday. I went to it and sat in the audience, listening. There were few people in the audience who were not also reading, and only readers managed to sit through the whole thing. The readers and me, that is. I listened and listened. I didn't care if it was good or bad. I learned from everything. Then I went to every reading I could for the next ten years. When I was in Minneapolis that meant about five a week.

Looking back, I don't know where that flame inside me came from, but it is good to remember it when I find myself even today sitting inside the Garden Restaurant on the plaza with no windows near my booth. It is one of the first warm days after a cold winter; it is afternoon and I find myself here writing in my notebook when I want to go outside and play instead. It is good to remember how I got here in the first place and how this all came about, how wild my young love was for writing.

About a month ago, I spent some time with Geneen Roth, who has written three books on compulsive eating. I was musing to her how I thought that my whole life of writing was an addiction, that I had given up home, lovers, a normal life for it.

She listened to me for a while, this woman who knew the ins and outs of food obsession and compulsion. Then she said, "No, Natalie, an addiction diminishes you. You have not been diminished by writing. It is your passion."

Oh, my passion! That is what finally carried me through. Let passion burn all the way, heating up every layer of the psyche, the conscious and the unconscious. Otherwise, you'll be like me with tennis—willing to drop it at sixteen when a boyfriend came along. Get tougher than that. Don't let anything take it away.

Try this:

Write about something you really loved, a time when you felt whole and complete in an activity all for itself. It could be something as simple as learning to make a grilled cheese sandwich, or a time your uncle taught you to tie your shoelaces into a bow. Something you concentrated on as a kid because the ability to concentrate is where the bliss and love come from. Be specific but don't forget to throw in a detail about a cloud out the window as you bent to tie the shoe or the chandelier above your head as you leaned down. This is good practice. While you concentrate and narrow in, you are also aware of the whole world.

43

Pleasure

A writer I know who is now in her sixties told me that in her late twenties, she had a nervous breakdown because she didn't know who she was. She moved to New York City from the rural South, and she was estranged from her family. She wandered down Thirty-fourth Street, completely lost. She said she found a therapist who slowly, over three years, saved her life. In the very first session of her therapy, the therapist asked her to find one thing that she liked, just for herself, not because her mother said it was good or the South said it was good or because she wanted to impress a New Yorker. Finally, by the end of the hour, she came up with one thing. She knew, irretrievably, just for herself, that she honestly liked the taste of chocolate. From that one pleasure, she and the therapist began the construction of an authentic life.

I dare to say that literature is built on such pleasure. Let's put school, exams, criticism aside. The actual act of reading a good book is a pleasure. Miriam said, "When you read a book, you're not creating karma." You have stepped out of trouble, out of cause and effect. You are just there with legs swinging over the arm of a chair, your eyes on a page, your mind connecting with the mind of the author who wrote a book once upon a time.

It is good to begin from this place, for us to notice what brings us true pleasure. It is a good foundation for writing. It will carry us further than if our work is fed by anger, revenge, jealousy or hate. I am not saying we should avoid writing about these things. I am saying, let the furnace of writing be fueled by what pleases us, so as we write about rage or destruction, we don't get stuck there. The world is bigger than that.

I heard Linda Leonard, who wrote *The Wounded Woman* (Shambhala, 1983) and *On the Way to the Wedding* (Shambhala, 1987), speak in Santa Fe about a year ago. She was working on a new book about creativity and addiction. She said that the artist and the alcoholic have parallel paths. They both go into the darkness, but the alcoholic gets stuck there. The artist (if she is not also addicted) goes into the darkness and is transformed by the experience and comes out more alive. I picture the artist as someone deep-sea diving, holding her breath and bursting out of the water into the air six minutes later, one hundred feet from where she began, with sun catching the water spray. The alcoholic dives down and gets caught in the sludge or is mesmerized by the underwater world and drowns. The good thing is that the artist can move through experience, learn from it and not be caught by it. Writing and reading can give us this.

The first time I did a meditation retreat, in 1976, I remember the meditation teacher explaining that insanity was getting stuck in a thought and not being able to let it go—"I'm crazy, I'm crazy, I'm crazy." The tape inside doesn't stop or we don't go on to the next thought—"I'm crazy, I want to eat a hamburger, my nose itches, I wish I owned a horse." When we go from thought to thought, we might sound crazy, but we're moving on, not being frozen by one idea. So maybe one deep pleasure is movement: giddyup, get along there, write one word, then another, turn that page.

A woman I met recently who has a creative writing degree from one of the best universities and is wonderful to talk to about literature said she began five novels and never finished one of them. I homed right in. "What happened?" I asked. "You mean you wrote ten pages and then quit?"

"No," she said. "I'd get to page one hundred and eighty, I'd be humming along and then, suddenly I'd lose interest or wouldn't believe in the story anymore. It carried me to page one eighty and then no farther."

I grew quiet. "It is an act of faith," I said. "It's going on when you no longer believe. It's walking right off into that wilderness." I was in the middle of my novel and I understood. I was busy dragging my ass through the desert myself.

Why don't you say that you are allowed one incomplete book, one time you give up and that's it. Otherwise, once you begin a book, no matter how much you hate it, you finish it. I think that is a good idea, because it makes your furnace burn strongly before you begin. You don't just grab an idea willy-nilly and run with it for four chapters and quit. Commitment is a matter of pleasure. Let it be deep pleasure. And wait till you are sure (well, as sure as you'll ever be), then plunge in and know you have to swim all the way from Montauk Point to Paris and you can't turn back. There's a wild and frightening pleasure in that.

Try this:

Make a list of what pleases you, all for yourself, not because your mom, your girlfriend, your aunt likes it. Be a little strict at first. "C'mon, Natalie, you can't put down racetracks. You only like them because your father did." But I can put down the way humidity appears on trees, or I could write about Mondays, Taos, a tall glass of water, the smell of barbecued chicken.

Now write for ten minutes about one pleasure on your list.

It is a very kind act to take a friend's hand and show him or her the pleasure you have in something. Write with this in mind, as though you were sharing it. My friend Cecile once taught me about the beauty of stones. She took me walking in an arroyo outside of Santa Fe and often bent and picked up a stone. "See, this color, the shape." I'd look, nod, and she put it down in place. We walked a little farther and she showed me another one. It took time. I didn't get it right away, but she was so kind I followed her. That is good to remember. She did not lift up a huge boulder and crack it over my head.

Don't demand that the reader like what you like. Begin slowly and gently and show your pleasure in something.

44

Horse Racing

I will tell you something. In some way you mustn't think it is true. You mustn't believe in it enough to think it will save your life and make you rich, but it is about writing. It is about writing's secret power that you must forget, that you must use only for writing. Do not squander it or become greedy.

Two summers ago in late August, I went with my friend Janet to the state fair in Albuquerque. They had horse races there, and I said to Janet, "Hey, let's buy tickets and go."

I was excited. It was the summer I had fallen in love with horses and I remembered my father always went up to the race track at Saratoga Springs in New York. I wanted to stand in the grandstand and just watch the big, beautiful animals race by.

Janet picked up a betting booklet listing the races, the horses' names, their histories. She said, "Let's bet. It's just two dollars for each race. We can chip in a dollar each."

"Okay," I said. "Let's see the racing form." We had come

in the middle of the second race. I looked at the list of twelve horses for the third race. I ran my finger down their names and I felt an energy, a little yanking, at the seventh horse's name. "Here, I want to bet on Thunder Bolt. Number seven. Let's bet to place. I'm not sure if he will be one, two, or three."

Thunder Bolt came in second. We won a little money. Janet wanted to bet again. She said, "We have a winning streak. I pick this time." She picked Gertrude Fly. She said that her boyfriend's cat was named Gertrude.

I said, "Okay," but I ran my finger down the list for the fourth race anyway and felt Sullivan's Trap had a calling. "Okay," I said. "It's your turn, but I bet number eight at least places."

Sullivan's Trap came in first.

Gertrude Fly came in last. Janet was disappointed. She tore up the ticket, bent her head and watched the torn paper flutter to the ground.

"Now it's my turn," I said. "C'mon, we only lost a dollar apiece in the last race." I ran my finger again down the list. It was number nine. "Let's bet on Arrowhead to show," I said.

"Oh, let's be brave," Janet said. "Let's bet for it to win."

I shook my head, but I gave in. All I knew was that Arrowhead would be either one, two, or three. I couldn't be sure it would be number one.

Arrowhead came in second and we lost, but Janet turned her head to me. "What do you think for the next?" She handed me the racing form.

I said, "Number two."

"To place, show, or win?"

I scrunched up my face. "I'm not sure. I only know it will be in the top three."

"Okay, how about number two. Place?"

"Okay."

Wizard's Hunch came in third. We lost. I had enough. I wanted to get out of there. "Let's go," I said.

Janet was looking at me. "How do you know this stuff?"

I took her elbow and wheeled her through the crowd. "I don't know," I said. Then I thought to myself, "Where'd you ever get the idea to look down the list and trust some kind of energy you felt?" It made me nervous. I thought I was becoming a medium. Extraterrestrials would be using my mouth to speak through and I'd go hungry for a peanut butter sandwich.

Then I realized: It was writing. I'd learned long ago, so long ago I'd forgotten I knew it, to trust those perceptions at the periphery of my mind. When we write, many avenues or directions open up in us and I have learned to go for the words that call me, that have a shivering possibility. It's not something I think about. I submerge myself in the pond of darkness and let the electrical animals of thought pass by. If we are awake, the whole world is shimmering and giving us guidance. I was awake at the race track because the horses' names were written down. I have trained myself in one area: To be awake to words.

So writing can teach you many things. To learn the act of writing is to obtain magical powers. They are a secret. No one can give them to you. You must work at them yourself. And do not abuse it. I used the five dollars I made from our first bet minus the three dollars I lost on the three following races to buy a two-dollar raffle for a boy's club annual fund drive. And that raffle ticket brought me nothing. I didn't win the bike, the TV, or the hundred dollars' worth of groceries. So there you have it. Empty at the beginning and empty at the end—the old story you learn over and over as a writer.

Try this:

Write about a time you had magical powers; you might have to go back to childhood. Or write about dreams or wishes you've had for magical powers. Give those powers to yourself and write from that place.

Now write for ten minutes, without thinking, take a leap— who are your angels? Name them all. Go.

Try this:

Bite into a piece of celery. Write down a strong word. Not like *tasty*, *salty*, *good*. Sit still and wait for a concrete word to come: *tiger*, *muscle*, *glass*. The strong word does not have to be logical. It should not be an ordinary, conditioned response. For instance, if I say "love," try to think of something other than *valentine*, *heart*, *forever*. Go to a deeper level, below discursive thought, to the first way your mind flashes on something. Stay with concrete nouns that give pictures: love— *avocado;* love—*hemisphere;* love—*gasoline*.

Smell a rose. Smell it as though you never before knew rose, flower, petal. Smell it for the first time. Jot down strong words. Again, stay concrete: rose—*liver;* rose—*barley;* rose— *river water*. If a strong memory or phrase or picture comes up, write it down.

This is how good comparisons are made. You smell a rose and go out to the periphery of your perceptions and trust them; catch something beyond ordinary thought and reel it in. Let me try to take "rose: *liver*" further. "This rose smells like liver sizzling in a frying pan. The smell shoots through my nose and breaks open my lungs like a plaster wall collapsing under a wrecking ball." This comparison is different from "the rose smells sweet," "it's a pretty smell." It has solid images: liver, frying, plaster walls, wrecking ball. Writing is a visual art. Check that your writing has pictures.

Sit with a friend or a group of people. Take turns throwing out words: *window*, *chair*, *horse*, *brick*, *ceiling*, *ice cream*, *Cadillac*, *hill*, *London*, *soup*.

After each word, allow a minute for the group to jot down strong words. This is good practice. It carries us deeper than the school compositions we wrote about our vacation: "It was fun. It was nice. I liked it." It carries us below what we think we are supposed to say to what it was really like. It makes things snap. Now take it further than *London* and your strong word for it: *aluminum foil.* Bam! a picture. "In March, I visited England for the first time. The weather was cold and the wind brittle. I walked the streets of London and the city felt like crushed aluminum foil below the dirty soles of ten thousand feet."

Be patient. You don't immediately or always hit home with terrific, strong concrete words. Often it takes a little warm-up time to feel you blasted through to something alive and on the mark. Jump in.

45

Success

After *Writing Down the Bones* came out, I called my parents in Florida.

"Mom, Leonard Cohen's manager called me. He said he liked the book," I told her long distance.

"Who's Leonard Cohen?" my mother asked.

"He's a famous songwriter," I explained. I couldn't impress her.

"Well, at least he's Jewish," my father chimed in on the extension phone.

This past April I did a workshop in South Carolina. I invited my parents to drive up and sit in. I hoped this time they would understand my success. Registration for the workshop was at seven Friday evening. The actual workshop began at seven-thirty. Since my plane arrived at five-thirty, I asked to be taken to my hotel to shower. Everyone at the workshop registered and milled around, wondering where I was. My parents were seated on a couch in the corner.

My picture is on the back of the *Bones* book. Someone spotted my mother. My mother and I resemble one another. My mother is in her seventies and I am forty. The woman who saw my mother nudged someone else. They looked from the book cover to my mother on the couch and then back again. "That must be her," they decided. One of them shook her head. "This picture must have been taken years ago."

"Writing's a hard life," the other laughed.

When I arrived, I wore clothes I had worn six months earlier when I visited my parents in Florida. In Florida, they hated the pants and jacket. At the workshop, the first thing my father said was, "I love your outfit and your hair looks terrific." My hair had just been cut very short and usually they don't like that. But suddenly at the workshop, I could do no wrong.

During breaks, people came up to my parents and asked, "Who does she take after?"

My father responded, "My wife and I are really very ordinary people. She did this all herself."

To my amazement my parents not only sat in on the whole weekend, they also did all the writing assignments. At the end of one assignment, my father waved his hand wildly when it was time to read.

I wanted to ignore him, but finally I had to choose him. He read about me, how we stopped at the race track on the way home from college after my freshman year, and how I started to cry that I wanted to go home. He announced that he composed the whole thing in his head lying in bed in the hotel the night before. I stood in front of the room as he read, feeling ridiculous.

When he was done, what could I say? "Good." I nodded. I turned my head. "Who else would like to read?"

"Wait a minute! Did you really like it?" he asked.

"Yes, it had a lot of detail." I paused. "Unfortunately," I added. Everyone laughed.

When we went out to dinner that night, my parents were all praise. I was increasingly uncomfortable, but I couldn't say why. They loved all my outfits; they said they were actually learning things about writing.

On Sunday the workshop was over and we planned to drive to Charleston for two days to visit with each other and see the city. In the car, driving through the green rolling hills, suddenly my father wished I hadn't worn the shorts I was wearing.

They imitated the way I talked during the workshop. "You know, how the mind moves," my father said, his hands on the steering wheel and my mother's hands flying in the air, the way I had used my hands in the workshop to explain the movement of the mind.

When we arrived at the 1890 bed-and-breakfast I had booked us in, my father was worried there was no air conditioning and he wanted to know where the elevator was. My mother gave me two pink cotton nightgowns, a present they'd brought from Florida.

As it neared dinnertime, I was increasingly depressed and lonely, but I could not say why. After all, hadn't I been successful, hadn't they seen it? We changed for dinner. I walked out in one of the nightgowns my mother had just given me. I wore a leather belt around it and a pair of huaraches on my feet. My father didn't notice. My mother's face fell and she bit her lip. At the restaurant, when I excused myself for a moment, my mother told my father about the nightgown. When I returned to the table, my father said, "Your mother tells me you're wearing the nightgown we just brought you for a gift."

"Yes, I am," I agreed and took a sip of water, then peered at the large menu and we ordered dinner.

Now it is September, several months later. I understand something now that I didn't then. Success is different from love. I mixed them up. I thought if I wrote a book I'd get the attention I had wanted a very long time ago from my parents for just being alive and being myself. That wasn't the only reason I wrote. I wrote because I never felt so whole and alive as I did when I wrote my first poem. I was complete. I created something from myself and nothing was wanting. That was the original flame. It was good enough, but along the way I mixed it all up. I thought it could heal the world; it could heal me; it could do everything, because I felt so good when I wrote. I took one step ahead of the ordinary good act of writing. I wanted to become successful, noticed, famous, so I could finally get the love and attention I didn't get as a child.

I took writing outside writing. I took my life outside life. I wanted to throw it way ahead of me, thinking it would cure something way behind me. "If I get famous, then . . . ," "If I get this book finished, then . . . ," "If I win this grant, then . . . ," "If I get published, then . . ."

We need to let writing be writing and let it give us what it gives us in the moment. If we connect with anything in the moment, it frees us of the past, present, and future. We are just there. If we are chopping wood, we are chopping wood; brushing our teeth, brushing our teeth; walking, walking.

When I write a book, I am eager for it to be finished. That is stupid. It's too long to wait. And what do I think will happen when it is finished? I'll write another book—I'm a writer. So finally we have to forget expectation. Just write. It's its own goodness. Success makes you ridiculous; you end up wearing nightgowns to dinner.

46

White Castles

*I*t was a Monday night. Renée and I were teaching a two-hour workshop in the old Mabel Dodge Luhan house in Taos. The topic was Raw and Enduring: The Writer's Life. Renée taught the first hour: timed writing exercises about rawness. Then I got up. I felt like the old patriarchy: enduring.

I told them, "It doesn't matter what you write in this workshop, what counts is that you continue."

Someone shot up a hand: "Yeah, but isn't timing important, too? You might be ready to publish, but the people you wrote about are still alive. Don't you have to wait so you don't hurt them?"

It seemed obvious that something was wrong with that question. You can't sit around and wait for people to die. I flung off my long beard and white robe of the old school, the starter of writing practice, and told them a story from my life right then.

"Well, I don't think you can wait around for the right time.

When's the right time? Two weeks ago I decided I had to tell my father I was going out with women. My parents are like the original Zen mind. They go out in the world and everything is new to them: tape recorders, video cameras.

"I called them long distance, and my father said, 'Nat, I was in the library! I found this thick book. It said it had listed all the books that were ever published.'

"He must have found *Books in Print*. No big deal. Every bookstore has it, but to my father it was a phenomenon.

" 'Well, I thought I'd look you up. They didn't have you. So then I had an idea. I'd look it up by title. Sure enough, there you were! I got so excited, I ran over to the librarian to show her. She said if I brought your book in, they'd put a sign in the front cover that I donated it. I ran to the bookstore and bought one and brought it in. Nat, I was so proud!'

"I hesitated. My mother, who was on the extension, said, 'Nat, is something wrong? You're not talking.'

"This was my opening. I walked through. 'Dad, have you noticed that I haven't mentioned men in the last year?'

"My mother, who already knew, gasped, 'Oh, my God. No, Nat, no!' I kept going.

"When I was done, my mother said, 'This was some time to tell us.'

"When would have been the perfect time? Never. You can't wait for that. You have to go ahead."

I smiled at the class. "I guess you want to know what my father said?" I paused. "He asked me why I was telling him.

"I told him, 'I don't want to keep things hidden.'

"He said, 'You know I like to be kept in the dark.' "

We spend a lot of time holding up the white castles of our parents or society. These have nothing to do with ourselves or with the truth. Holding them up is a great burden. They're not real castles anyway—more like the fake plaster castles of the cheap hamburger chain. My parents have already made their lives. This is *my* life now. I have to live it. If I say the truth and am condemned for it, then something is wrong. Yes, there are many truths, but I should be free to say mine. We are not encouraged to do that. And our society is in denial, too, so of course it is hard to say what you see as a writer and not feel crazy, not worry that you should wait until the perfect moment. We have to make the perfect moment. We can't wait around.

This is a story that Katagiri Roshi told in his Wednesday-night lecture after I was at the Zen center for one year:

"A father and son were out fishing in a rowboat in the ocean. The father fell in the water and couldn't swim. At that moment, the son had a great longing to enter a monastery and realize the truth. He rowed to shore." End of story. I was used to Zen stories being like that—they just ended—but this was too much.

I shot up my hand. "Wait a minute, Roshi. What about the father? What happened to him?"

Roshi looked straight ahead. "He drowned."

I paused. "What kind of religion is this, anyway?"

For a long time, I thought about that story. I didn't get it. Now I understand.

But I will admit, walking down Morada Lane, the day after the Raw and Enduring workshop, looking out at Taos Mountain and the cottonwoods in the last days of August, I thought kindly of my father and his original mind that discovered *Books in Print* as a colossal new phenomenon.

I remembered one time when I was visiting my parents in December. It was the last day I was there and my father wanted to take my mother and me to his favorite place for breakfast. My father was very excited.

During the whole breakfast, he kept pushing forward the

pink plastic tablecloth and looking underneath the table. At the end of the meal, after the waitress left us the bill, he looked under the table again. My mother and I both were wearing sandals. "You know," he said, addressing me and my mother, "if someone just showed me your feet, I'd never figure out you were related to me." He shook his head.

After remembering this, I caught myself thinking, "Now when do you think he'll die? I can't hurt him and publish anything." I laughed. I was brave the night before, told everyone to go for it, and the next day my kind heart didn't want to hurt anyone's white castle. There you have it. We're human beings. My writing self is braver than the rest of me. I follow her, trust her, but I know my human self, the part of me that is not a warrior of truth and words, lags behind. We have to take it all into consideration.

I was in a café in Paris last March, writing hard for a full morning. I wrote about lesbian bars. When I was done, my human self whined. "Oh, no, Nat. We're not going to publish that, are we?"

My writer self turned to her, incredulous. "Of course we are. What's the problem? It came through us, we'll say it."

Yes, I will always be true to my writer self. She is very brave and fearless, but I've learned she doesn't care about anything else, like my health, my contentment, my well-being. I used to follow her blindly and leave the rest of me homeless, shoeless, and hungry. Now I work to care for all of me, so when I do publish the truth, I'll have a life to stand on, to steady me when I bring to light the deepest secrets of my soul.

47

Crossing Boundaries

On a Sunday night three years ago on Don Cubero Street, in a thick-walled adobe house, I finished writing *Writing Down the Bones*. The book took one and a half years to write, not counting twelve years of teaching writing workshops and developing writing practice. For the last seven weeks of creating the book, I wrote all day, seven days a week. I was in an altered state. I went to bed early. I woke up early. I ate well. I even dressed in quiet colors and I didn't socialize at all. If anyone were to look at me from the outside, I appeared rather dull, but inside I felt wild.

The moment I pulled the last page of *Bones* out of the typewriter, I said, "Nat, I think you're done with the book." The next thing that shot through my head was, "And I want to be with women now." I jerked my head around. "Huh?" It was a great leap. It was not something I had particularly contemplated before.

It took me a year to digest it. On my way to Europe that

September, stopping in Manhattan on the way, looking out at the Hudson River from the fortieth floor of a friend's apartment, I asked, "Okay, Nat, what's up? What's going on with you?"

"I want to explore women," I answered.

"Okay, you've got it. Two full years. Go for it," I said to myself.

I bought a book called *The Gaia Guide to Europe*, listing gay nightspots, resorts, etc., and I landed in Madrid. At night, I walked the narrow, haunted streets of cobblestone with a lamplight far in the distance, looking for obscure addresses of lesbian bars. Usually, the bar had no sign out and you had to ring a bell to be let in. I went to those bars in Madrid, Barcelona, and Paris. In Lisbon, I couldn't find any.

In the daytime I read Hemingway's *Death in the Afternoon*, a thick technical book about bullfighting. I fell in love with Hemingway that month and wanted to become a matador.

So here I was at night, stalking some kind of darkness I imagined I could find in a women's bar, and in the hot afternoons I entered the male world of matadors and bull rings. I rode on trains through the high yellow hills of Spain, devouring a book by an American male writer whom I admired. I wanted his precision and clarity in a foreign country in the face of gore and blood. That month was one of the best times I ever had in my life. I was alive in all the contradictions. I didn't try to put things in neat categories and patterns. I just was alive.

Writing practice teaches us that. To go out there in the wilderness and make friends with it. I'm not saying we all have to become lesbians in order to write or that we have to be black, a Jew, or an Indian to have compassion for another person, but we do have to be willing to enter wild mind, where everything exists and where we are not separate from a horse, bird, Vietnamese, Chinese, gay person, pebble, or redneck. Writing practice takes us to a place where boundaries melt.

You taste impermanence. When I'm writing without stopping, it is as though I am writing on water. There is no thought I can hold onto, no concept that covers everything. One image melts into another.

When I decided that I wanted to be with women, it was about boundaries and crossing over boundaries. The only thing that matched the wildness I felt inside when I wrote was kissing a woman. When I did it, it felt wild, but also wholesome and ordinary, not such a big deal. It made me wonder what other life-affirming and positive things my middle-class background had programmed me against.

Once in a twelve-step program, I brought up the topic of wildness. A man who is now a musician said he was brought up in Pittsburgh, and his parents never allowed him to go to the black section of town. When he was sixteen, he and three of his high-school buddies went to a jazz bar there. It was the first time he had ever heard jazz. He said he'd never felt so alive and happy. The next morning at breakfast, he was so excited he told his parents about it. They were upset that he went there and said jazz was awful. As he lifted his scrambled eggs to his mouth, he had the first inkling that his parents could be wrong about the world.

Sometimes I have students make lists of forbidden themes, things they are afraid to look at or talk about. It is surprising what they list as forbidden. Mostly the themes stem from childhood and are the simple truths of people's lives: a father's alcoholism, the death of a grandmother, how much something costs, the age of a mother, who got divorced, a black person in the classroom, being afraid of the dark.

What I found in being with women and in the lesbian bars were wider possibilities for being a woman. I stepped out of the heterosexual world with its confines for both men and women and got a vision of space, where I could stretch in any direction. I went to the bars looking for other reflections of myself. I didn't know that then. It seemed wild and exotic. What I found were women who had made choices for themselves outside the norm. Being a writer in our society is making a choice, too, outside the norm.

Writing practice brings us back to the uniqueness of our own minds and an acceptance of it. We all have wild dreams, fantasies, and ordinary thoughts. Let us feel the texture of them and not be afraid of them. Writing is still the wildest thing I know.

A man last night in a meeting I went to said he has a job he loves, a wife who is pregnant with their second child, a son who just entered kindergarten and seems to like it, and still he wakes up depressed. He said he looks around him and knows his life is good. I sat there and felt great compassion for him. This is human life. Sometimes nothing makes sense. No one way contains it all.

I understand why a lot of writers drink heavily or shoot themselves. When you write, you tap the core of your wildness, you have to be prepared to let that live inside you and not destroy it. It is scary to tell you I have slept with women, but what kind of a person would I be to encourage you to write the truth and then not tell the truth myself? And what kind of friend would I be to my sisters? and my brothers? And most of all, what kind of real compassion would I show myself? Writing is a great journey. It is a path with the possibility of making us free. And to tell the truth, it can do all of this while you sit at a desk, your hand moving across the page, while you look ordinary, even a little boring in dull colors with not much animation on your face.

Paris Notebook

*L*ast night I was with the president of a big American company and his wife. They are both friends of mine. Carol was there too. I insisted we take the subway and visit every café Hemingway wrote in and have a drink in each one. It was the time of the bombings, and my friends did not want to take the subway. They were very nervous, but I made them. We went to the Select first. The tables reached all the way out on the wide sidewalk to the street. The street was Montparnasse. Across the way was the Cupole, and farther down was the Dôme.

I told my friends at the Select about matadors and *Death in the Afternoon*. Then they were tired and did not want to continue with me to the other cafés. We hugged good-bye and I went on to the Closeries des Lilas, but I was not alone. Hemingway was with me. If you love a writer enough, have stepped into his books and therefore his mind, he is never dead for you. In real life, I don't know how much we'd have to say to each other—"Hey, Hem, you should see the tiger I shot last week in Brooklyn." But in that quiet place where tombstones mark time with eternity, Ernest and I know each other. Our hands are around thick coffee mugs, and we sit across from each other and say nothing.

49

Dark and Light

A small painting of van Gogh's just sold to a Japanese collector for fifty million dollars. Van Gogh died insane and penniless at thirty-seven years old. I stood in the rain outside the Musée d'Orsay in Paris for two hours to see an exhibit of his work. My hands were getting cold. It was early March. If van Gogh could only see this now, I thought to myself. The line reached way down a long city block. The Seine was across the street. The show covered the ten years van Gogh was in Paris (1878–88). I read Jean Rhys, an English author, to make the time go faster as I stood in line. Rhys wrote about broken women who drank and were lost, moved from hotel to boarding house in London and Paris. Her characters, like herself, were alcoholic, and things did not get better. Rhys wrote about darkness. I'd been interested in darkness for a while and had been wanting to claim my own, but I was not sure what it was.

It all began on an early July evening in Minneapolis three

summers ago. Kate and I were eating at Brenda's on the corner of Third Street and First Avenue. We had just seen a perfect sunset on the Mississippi and she was treating me to dinner.

"What do you think about light and dark?" I asked her as I reached for a glass of water.

"I don't know. What's dark?" She scratched her chin and raised her right eyebrow.

The waitress served us shrimp in butter with rice.

"Friendship—is it dark or light?" I flashed back.

She sat at attention. "Dark. Yes, dark. Very scary," she said.

"Yeah, I think so, too," I said. "How about love?"

"Light," she hesitated. "Light and dark."

"Minnesota?"

"Dark. Real dark."

"Watermelon?"

"Light."

"Death?"

"Light and dark."

"Writing?"

"Dark. Dark and light."

Rivers? Russia? hope? monastery? Buddha? wind? dream? Dark, dark, dark, dark, dark, dark.

As we talked more, dark transformed. Dark became good *and* bad. It became energetic, fertile, less scary, more desirable.

I hung out in bars all one winter in Taos, New Mexico, wanting to find darkness. Instead, I was bored. I noticed that the people who drank a lot repeated the same things over and over. They said a brilliant line, a deep line, for instance, "Death enters Taos every winter." They shook their heads. I was intrigued, but it went no further. They said nothing else.

They repeated that same line. Maybe there was nothing else to say about death and winter and Taos.

One night two drunk Indians from the pueblo got into a fist fight at the bar and flung each other over tables. This went on for a while until a waitress dared to stop them. The waiters stood back. I thought of Hemingway, Jack Kerouac. I thought of the pain of writing. I thought it was more painful never to write. I couldn't find what I was looking for in bars, and the smoke got to me.

By the time I stood in line with Jean Rhys as company, I was familiar with the darkness in her characters. It was the frozen darkness I saw in the Taos bars, but her writing caught it like broken glass. It was finally my turn to pay my twenty francs and go in.

There was a wall of early van Goghs, then a painting by Toulouse-Lautrec. At first I was confused. I couldn't read French well. As I went along I realized you couldn't have a show of van Gogh during that time without showing his friends, those he was inspired by. All of them were living in Paris; they cross-fertilized one another. Next to an oil of the Clichy Bridge by van Gogh was a charcoal of the same bridge by Paul Signac. A nude couple with the man seated: the side view drawn by Emile Bernard, the front view in pencil by van Gogh. "To my friend Lucien Pissarro" was written on a painting of a plate of apples, and a drawing by Pissarro of two men sitting next to each other talking was entitled *Vincent in Conversation*. I turned another corner; a Monet painting of a flowering apple tree near a stream, next to van Gogh's *Spring in the Woods*. Everything was interconnected.

I walked around thinking, "And all this while, he was only a few steps away from madness." A painting of three pairs of shoes, another of French novels—a tribute to the French writers he loved. He was connected not only to painters but to writers. I went back two rooms and slowly viewed again the paintings I had just seen. His solitariness coexisted with his camaraderie. The first two rooms of paintings climaxed with *Femme dans un jardin*. Woman in a garden. The painting was full of light. He caught exactly how it was to be in tall grass, with the woods behind you and the sun on the green blades, how the blades became translucent. The whole scene was luminous, alive with light. Van Gogh himself must have swallowed summer in order to paint this. "He knew the light," I said to myself over and over as I looked over the crowded shoulders of the other viewers. No one spoke English. I was alone. I had become an artist, a writer. I had wanted it so badly. Now I had it. I had no family. Van Gogh never sold a painting while he was alive. He died poor and crazy and all the while he held inside the knowledge of light, of color.

"I don't have to seek the darkness anywhere but in myself," I thought. "I have enough, if I let it out, to be Berlin during World War II." We are always one step from destruction. My car was stolen right before I left for Europe. It would take all my savings to get another. I realized I have no income but writing. How much can I think to say? And will people want to read it? And what a thin living it is! I became nervous being so close to van Gogh's brilliance and insanity. "I should get health insurance," I thought to myself. Who says my kidneys will work tomorrow? Sanity? Dark. Insanity? The same thing.

In the last self-portrait of the show, van Gogh painted his eyes bright green, even the whites of them. He was already mad. He knew so much light and ended in darkness. I left the Musée d'Orsay. It was very gray outside. I walked down rue de Raspail to Montparnasse cemetery. I needed quiet. I needed to sit near the grave of a dead poet. I thought it would help. It was 3:50. I had forty minutes to find a dead poet. The cemetery closed at 4:30. I wandered through section 15,

looking for Robert Desnos. The gravestones were close together and many were very old. Flat against the fence of the
cemetery were high-rise apartments where the living could
look over the dead. I could not find Robert Desnos. If I could
only find one dead poet, I would be okay, I thought to myself.
I would sit by his gravestone.

By accident, I found Jean-Paul Sartre and Simone de Beauvoir. They never married, but they were buried together. I sat
down on the green bench next to them. I placed a small stone
on their grave. I learned that gesture in Israel. It means, I
have visited. I just sat there. What to say? Nothing. Nothing.
Simone de Beauvoir lived in an apartment across from Montparnasse cemetery a good part of her life. Then she was
buried in it. I was told that she and Sartre wrote for two hours
every morning in the Fifties in Aux Deux Magots, the café
where I go to write whenever I am in Paris.

Finally, I spoke to de Beauvoir in her grave. "Simone," I
said aloud, "I repeat to my students your line from the *Second
Sex*." Then I recited it to her. " 'In order to be an artist, one
must be deeply rooted in the society.' "

I lay in bed that night in the hotel. "I have just turned
forty," I said to myself. "What do you want by the time you
are fifty?"

And I answered immediately, without thinking, "I want to
love someone and care about them."

"Not write books? Not be famous? Rich?" I asked.

"That is good, too. But most of all I want to love someone
and care about them," I answered.

Try this:

Write about towns and cities you have passed through and places you stayed in a week or less.

Write about a car trip. Go. Write about trains. Go. Write about a hotel you stayed in. Go. Make up twenty of your own travel topics. Explore different dimensions of your travels.

50

Orchestra

*I*n the late 1970s, I taught reading in the Minneapolis public schools. I taught it to ninth-graders who read at second-grade reading level. It was a special federally funded program, so the student-teacher ratio was one to one. For a full hour I worked with one student. We sat together and we read aloud simple stories of high interest about motorcycle races and great basketball players. We also slowly went over lists of simple words that were often used in these stories—*their, even, because, wheel, motor*—and we recited consonants, vowels, and consonant blends from flash cards.

One day in December, Philip turned to me after we had laboriously gone over one page for a half hour, shook his head, and said, "Miz Goldberg, you sure is patient. How do you listen to me so long?"

I smiled and said, "I want to help you."

Now that was true, but there was something else. I was a writer and I'd never before had the opportunity to pay such close attention to words. Leaning over Philip's shoulder, reading as he read, I felt how vowels carry the breath and use the breath to make different sounds. A-E-I-O-U and sometimes Y. Philip and I often said the vowels slowly one after the other. It felt like a riff on a sax. I experienced my lungs as bagpipes, my breath as a musical instrument.

I felt the consonants, too. They cut off the breath. They signaled the pause and the sound the pause made: for example, the letter *t* is more abrupt than *th*, which cuts the breath more softly. Leaning over Philip's shoulder, I experienced each word as a musical entity, and a full sentence as a musical score. We made music in reading words. When I read the word *balloon*, I wandered around in a whole world of sound. *Balloon* expanded and contracted. It was psychedelic.

From this understanding, I also looked at punctuation. A period was a heavy anchor for Philip, and he stopped and rested when he reached one. Punctuation had real significance. It signaled the beginning and end of thought.

"And if punctuation is about thought," I thought, "then in order to punctuate, we have to know our mind, to know what we think, and when one thought stops and the other begins. We have to understand the journey of thought, how thought moves around in our mind."

I sat there one day in that classroom with a geranium plant blooming in the window, this time leaning over Clarissa's shoulder, and I realized, "Why, in order to write a good sentence, we have to become Zen masters, we have to understand our minds!"

Then I thought about how our teachers in elementary school taught us to put commas after each word in a series, and I wondered if they realized how deep that was. What kind consideration it entailed. "I bought bologna, marmalade, gum, scissors, and a notebook at the store." The comma is asking us to pause after each purchase, to hold for a moment the dignity of each thing-ness. *Bologna*—a whole object, a whole thought in the mind, a visual picture. Yes. Then *gum* with a comma after it. Pause and feel its own solid being.

Knowing the weight and significance of vowels, consonants, punctuation, allows us more maneuverability with our breath and thoughts in writing. We can write like a river and sail for a long sentence and then *boom!* stop and make a short quick sentence right next to it, like an otter popping its head out of that river. We can play with the length of breath and thought like the slide on a trombone.

There are two pages in *Death in the Afternoon* where Hemingway goes on in long sentences about the weather in Spain and about when he was in the war in Constantinople, and then like a fast U-turn on a highway, with no warning and no switch of paragraph, he makes a simple comment: "Seeing the sunrise is a fine thing." No fancy words. Boom! Yes, seeing a sunrise is a fine thing. Right in the middle of action, we stop and see something else, but it is not only Hemingway's words that convey this. It is also the measure of his breath and sentences that conveys it.

Language does not work only on the level of word meaning. Let's face it: What does *the* mean anyway, or *at* or *as*? There are often a lot of words in a sentence that have no visual picture or specific meaning. Language works also on the level of dreams, on the subconscious, through its music, sound, breath, texture. We should be aware of this as writers and use it.

Driving through the center of Martha's Vineyard on Middle Road with Miriam, I told her I wanted to spend a year in

Paris. She was in the driver's seat, which was unusual. She turned from the steering wheel and said, "Your French is terrible. Come on, the truth. How long did you study French? Two years in high school?"

"No," I said. "I studied it every year from sixth grade through twelfth. And then four semesters in college." I smiled. "But every year all I learned to do was conjugate the verb 'to be.' "

Then I recited for her "I am," "you are," "she and he is," etc., in French. I even mixed that up and we laughed.

Thinking back now, it wasn't so dumb to know deeply the verb "to be." In knowing that, I knew sound, vowel, consonants, and how another language formed a significant verb. I could stand on the rue de Rivoli "being." I could repeat over and over, "Je suis, je suis." I would know two French words well: a noun and a verb. "I am." That is a good foundation. Before long, I could make a sentence. I could extend it to a full thought. "Je suis un cheval." "I am a horse." I could extend my consciousness through thought into an animal's. I could do all this in someone else's country in another language with pigeons at my feet and high gray slate roofs above my head. I could make a whole new orchestra of sound with a capital letter at the beginning of the sentence to signal its onslaught: "Je suis un cheval!"

The next morning, still feeling excited about language, I went out on the sun deck and opened *The Beet Queen*, by Louise Erdrich, a novel I was in the middle of reading. Each word felt voluminous and powerful. I heard cymbals and drums. "Ever since they came with their cake full of bugs and their spicy sausages, I've taken to sleeping downstairs on the pool table." This was the first sentence I read in a new chapter. I could hardly get past it. By the time I got to the end of the paragraph, I was exhausted. There was so much: words and breath and thought and periods and commas, and it was in the English language, a language I could understand. There is a whole jungle of wild breathing animals in just one page of writing!

Try this:

Make a list of words you really like. It doesn't matter if you know the meaning of the word or not. It also doesn't matter if you like what the word means. For instance, I love the word *cucumber*, but I don't necessarily like to eat cucumbers. I like the word *bulimic*, though I don't want to eat a good meal and then vomit in the toilet.

Feel the dignity and integrity of each word you write down. Keep the list in your notebook and add to it from time to time. Read the list to a friend. Read it slowly and feel those words. You might want to read the list aloud to prepare yourself each day to write. If you meet a friend to write, take turns reading your lists aloud to each other and then begin to write. The writing doesn't have to be about the list. It is a way to become present to words, to recognize their value, and to slow you down.

Now make a list of ordinary words you use all the time and don't care about: *the, when, is, how, you, of, been*. Feel their dignity. Read the list aloud. Let these words too penetrate your mind so you don't just string them along to hold the ruby you're trying to get to at the end of a sentence. Words are the building blocks of writing. Be present with all of them.

Miriam, who was dyslexic as a child, said words were opaque to her, they were solid, she couldn't see through them to their meanings. She just saw the word, as though each one were a luminous animal. She stopped at each one and couldn't go on. Usually we read a paragraph for the meaning or the story, and individual words become transparent. Because of her dyslexia, each word for Miriam was its own individual object.

She did learn to read in fourth grade and grew up to become

a poet. Really, that is what a poet is: someone who loves words for themselves and sees their magic: *vanilla, croissant, mulberry, vivify, homeopathic, cremation, ignorant, Isis, supplemental, thus, nor, rigor mortis.* Feel words and their power; the way atoms are the unit of human bodies and trees, so words are the small units that make up sentences.

It is good to examine words and feel their dignity inside us like a breath or a heartbeat.

51

Resident Poet

*I*n 1979 I was the resident poet at Andersen Elementary School in Minneapolis. It was one of my all-time favorite jobs. It was a big elementary school in the inner city and had three types of classrooms. The old-fashioned kind: You sat in rows, you raised your hand, you got in line to go to the bathroom. Open classes: Four teachers with different learning stations and a hundred kids wandering around from one station to another in a huge space with no walls. And then there was a third kind of classroom; for the life of me, I don't remember what kind it was, but I did teach in it.

I was at Andersen three days a week for the whole school year. There were lots of Indian kids, black kids, and some white kids. They were all bused in and mixed together. My salary was paid through a federal grant. The idea was that kids who might not do well academically could do well in the arts, and so they would gain confidence and not act so berserk after being bused in from the other side of the city.

I walked into Ellen's cluster of fifth- and sixth-graders on my first day—it was one of the open classes: we called the teacher by her first name—and I had the kids write about some place they loved. Lenore wrote about the Chippewa reservation in northern Minnesota and about her auntie who lived up there. "I remember my auntie go out on a cold day and she kiss and hug the trees."

Being an old fool myself, I went wild when Lenore read this aloud. "Lenore, that is a beautiful poem. I love your aunt. Please read it again. I want to hear it one more time."

Lenore read it again. I loved it the second time just as much. When I left the class at the end of the hour, I thought Lenore must be the valedictorian.

Ellen grabbed me as I left. "There must be a mistake. Lenore is the worst kid in class. She's a troublemaker."

I looked at her askance. I shook my head. "She's a great poet," and I breezed off.

During lunch in the faculty room, I heard three of the teachers from that cluster chuckling together. I went over and sat with them.

Sam said, "I heard about your great poet." He shook his head. "Lenore's aunt must have been drunk. That's why she was kissing trees."

"Believe me," I said, "Lenore can write."

And Lenore proved me to be right. She wrote poems all during the week and had them ready for me when I came in to her group the next Tuesday. Her identity changed over the months from the troublemaker to the class poet.

Mr. Rudolf's class was third-graders. It was a traditional class. After I'd been there three months, Mr. Rudolf called me aside. "I had to stop a fight between Ernie and Lombard on the playground. They were really belting each other. When

I broke it up and got between them, I asked them, 'Hey, guys, what's all this about?'

"Lombard pointed accusingly at Ernie. 'Mister Rudolf, Ernie said that I ain't a poet. Can't everyone who wants be a poet? Can't they? Natalie said so.' "

"Well, we've just made history," I told Mr. Rudolf. "This is probably the first time in America that poetry was fought over during a public school recess."

That day, Lombard wrote a wonderful poem. He was a short kid but seemed huge when he recited it in front of the class. I still know it by heart:

> Chicken and the car
> won't go
> spells Chicago
> smells pretty good.

I gave him a thumbs-up. "Hey, that's a good short one. You know what Allen Ginsberg said, 'Write one great line and you'll be famous. Write a long poem that's no good and you'll put people to sleep!' "

Lombard said he better read it aloud one more time, because it was short. I said, "Go for it."

At the end of the year, I did a ritual with the kids in Mr. Rudolf's class. We all wrote poems to the end of winter. We collected the last signs of winter—old wet leaves, small dead branches—and put them in plastic bags with their poems. Then I passed out Hershey chocolate kisses. We all had to put them on our tongues at the exact same moment; otherwise, the ceremony wouldn't work. We closed our eyes and said, "Farewell to cold." Then we attached our baggies to helium balloons and carried them outside. At the count of three, the whole class let them go. The balloons lifted imme-

diately and took off. The kids went mad and ran after them
to the end of the playground. They were screaming at the top
of their lungs. In truth, so was I and so was Mr. Rudolf.

I tell you this because having writers in the schools works.
I never taught the kids so-called children's literature. There
is some good children's literature out there, but there is a lot
that is condescending. Kids want the real stuff. I taught them
William Carlos Williams, Richard Hugo, D. H. Lawrence's
poem, "The White Horse." I showed them work by other
kids their age. This gave them the feeling that they, too,
could do it. I spoke straight to them. I told them what I liked
and how I became a writer. Kids are smart. They can get
things directly. I brought in the fall volume of Japanese haiku
by R. H. Blyth and read aloud from the greats: Basho, Shiki,
Issa, Buson.

"Did you feel the leaps?" I asked.

Yes, they nodded.

I told them what I knew about the writers I read them, so
the writers became real people. When I was in school, we
never learned anything about the writer. Knowing about the
writer helps to lead someone into their work. It makes a
connection.

I remember Mr. Di Francesco in my ninth grade. He was
teaching us American history. It was so boring! But one day,
out of the blue, while he was writing dates on the board, he
turned around and said, "I won't be here tomorrow. I'm
getting married this weekend." He shook his head. "Boy, is
there a lot to do in order to get married."

I woke right up, sitting in the first row, second seat. Mr.
Di Francesco was a human being! He had a life. That instant
is the only thing I remember of that whole year of American
history—not Columbus, not Vasco da Gama, but Mr. Di
Francesco, who was getting married and it was a hassle and for

a moment he revealed it. Everyone in that class was dying for human contact. That one moment when it happened, we all woke up. Then Mr. Di Francesco turned his back on us and wrote on the board 1492, and we were lost again in the oblivion of history.

I showed the kids at Andersen Elementary that writing was connected with their lives. I showed them how it was connected to my life and what it meant to me. That's how literature becomes alive. Watch an audience at a lecture. If the speaker is abstract and not present, our minds reflect that and drift off, too. If a lecturer speaks with original detail and is connected to his or her material, our minds will be present and we clue right in. The same principles of mind are at work in each individual. An alive teacher makes an alive classroom. It's as simple as that.

Understanding this as a writer is important too. You'll lose your reader if you are vague, not clear, and not present. We love details, personal connections, stories. Teaching and explaining things so the kids understood helped my own writing. I had to slow down, be specific, and speak the truth. Kids can be an acid test for your authenticity. They are not interested in your philosophy. They want the meat, the marrow, the bone. Teaching is practice in being real.

Try this:

Go ahead, kiss a tree. Walk right out your front door, put your arms around one that you pass every day at the curb, pucker up your lips and give it a big smacker.

Close your eyes and put a chocolate kiss in your mouth (or a strawberry or an almond, for those of healthful persuasion). Feel it on your tongue and dream.

Now write. Write anything you want. Kissing a tree is silly? What isn't silly? Writing's the silliest of all. If you can write out of that silliness, you'll be a long way on the path.

52

Detail

My mail piled up in my box at the Taos post office. I hadn't picked it up in a week. There was a big manila envelope. A kind student had sent me *Lovesick* (Harper & Row, 1987), poems by Gerald Stern. The cover was black and white with some red. It was an etching by David Hockney of a man riding a cooking spoon.

I took the book to the Garden Restaurant on the plaza and ordered—I'll admit it—bacon and French bread and a Coke. I opened the book and read "Steps," the last poem in the book. As I read the poem, the whole world opened up. I felt space. My teeth were happy hanging from my gums, my knees rested in my legs and my toes had their place. How could a poem do this? "It's poetry all over again," I thought to myself. That old primal cry for care and no care, words tossed from the throat and fallen to the page.

Gerald Stern's poem talked about steps, how stairs wear in the center if they're stone and splinter if they're wood. Then

I remembered steps: the ones at the New York City library on Fifth Avenue and the old stone ones up at Notre Dame.

Yeah, I thought, yeah.

I've always seen those steps but whoever thought to mention them? Gerald Stern did that for us and the world was now a little more alive and he made me a little more awake.

William Carlos Williams wrote a poem about standing by the water tap in his kitchen and waiting for it to freshen. You know city water: sometimes it comes out rusty and you wait for it to run clean. I've done it, but I never thought about it until I read Williams's poem.

Poetry is a dumb Buddha who thinks a donkey is as important as a diamond. Poetry is good practice for all the other writing we do, because it brings us back to where we are. It asks us to settle inside ourselves and be awake.

Miës van der Rohe, a twentieth-century architect, said God hides in the details. It is important as a writer to stay in the trenches with details and not jump out because it is scary to be there. Denial, repression, all those psychological adaptations we developed in childhood were ways of not being there, because being there was too painful. Writing demands that we cut through and be where we are and, like a cat gripping the side of a cement wall at the top of a ten-story building, stay there and look around and not blank out because it is too hard. This is it, here, whatever comes up.

The effect of a lot of popular drugs, including Ecstasy, LSD, peyote, is merely to make you open to the moment. "Wow, look at that salt shaker." You reach across the table and pick it up and notice the granules, shake some on your hand and put them on your tongue. Well, writing, when you sink into it, does the same thing. Even if you're writing about thirty years ago, you are completely there. Detail does this for us. Think about it. Life is not abstract. It is not good or bad. It is. A girl is not pretty. Our mind makes that judgment. The girl has red lips, white teeth, freckles brushed across her nose, eyes that hint at lilacs, and she just lifted her right eyebrow. The reader steps away and says she is pretty. The writer just stays with the eyes, the lips, the chin, and makes no judgments.

I am back at the Garden Restaurant. There are two tall glass salt-and-pepper shakers on my wooden table, a pottery bowl full of white packages of sugar. Three pats of butter sit in a white dish, and my favorite pen, the one that Pueblo Runner Printing hands out freely and generously, is lying on the table pointing to the big white plate with only one slice of French bread left and a slice of tomato lying on a piece of lettuce. These are original details. This is what is on this table. Now if you learn this deeply—what is in the present moment—you can transport it. "Hal is sitting in a steak house waiting for Sal. The waitress whizzes by, holding in her hand a white plate with a hamburger and lettuce with a thin slice of tomato on the side. The lettuce and tomato are about to fall over, they are so close to the plate's rim, but they don't, thanks to the adept grace of the red-haired waitress." See, there's that lettuce and tomato again, transported into your story. Having seen it once in the restaurant you were eating in (or writing in), it is yours. You can do what you want with it, and it has a ring of authenticity.

But all kinds of other wonderful things happen with original detail. A student in one class wrote: "My first beautiful boyfriend was missing three fingers and always smelled of baloney, because he lived above a butcher shop. My second boyfriend also smelled like baloney, but he did not live near a butcher shop." There is a mystery here. It is created by original detail. Put down what was—the butcher shop, and it holds what was not—no butcher shop and still the same smell. Something tells you about nothing. It is the power of the juxtaposition of detail.

Stay with what is and it will give you everything that isn't. From this wooden table I am leaning on, I can build a whole world of fiction.

Try this:

Okay. Just sit where you are sitting. Look around and take four minutes to describe it. By description, I don't mean "There's a *lovely* doily on top of a *well-made* table." Those two underlined words are your opinion. Just give the original details. "There's a white doily on top of a red Formica table. A woman in knee-high socks just walked by. She has a mole on her upper lip and the tip of her long braid brushes her leather belt."

Now have a person you know who is not actually in the restaurant enter and sit down and have lunch. Tell what he or she orders, what they are thinking about as they sip their water, where they come from, how they chew and swallow. Move in close. Watch them in your mind's eye, since they don't exist at the restaurant.

Now come out of your mind and describe the actual sky outside the restaurant window and tell what cars are passing by.

Now turn quickly back to your character. He is having a coughing fit. Help him or let him choke. Just let the story unfold, but keep grounding it in what you know, in where you actually are.

Naturally, you can be sitting in Taos and write about Brooklyn, but keep alive original detail, the detail as is, intermixed with your mind. We always have to ground our mind; otherwise, it has been known to blast off into space.

Try this:

At the top of the page, jot down the name of a river you know, a color, a city, a street, a fruit, a month, a job.

Now do a ten-minute timed writing, telling about the first time you made love, but as you write, you must include the above list in there some place. Just grab the words from your list helter-skelter as you go along.

This is a good exercise because it jolts you out of your usual way of writing about something. Most of us have known about the first time we made love for a long time. Suddenly, we have to talk about it with London, a pomegranate, blue, the Mississippi, April, Elwood Avenue, and carpentry thrown in. It jazzes it up and gives it a different dimension. It cuts through sentimentality and nostalgia to something bright, new, and clean. Fun, too.

Another good exercise is to make a list of things you fear and throw some of them in as you write about something you love. It grounds your writing, keeps you from sounding like a Pollyanna. It gives a larger dimension to what you love, because you embrace both emotions. It also intensifies what you love because of its juxtaposition to what you fear.

53

Earn the Right

You have to earn the right to make an abstract statement. You earn this right by using the concrete bricks of detail. After much original detail, you can take a little leap, step away, and make a statement: "Ah, yes, life is good," or "Life sucks." But you can't say "Life sucks" until you have given us a picture of it: a man lying in the gutter, mosquitoes feeding at his open sores, the tongue of his right shoe hanging out, his pockets turned inside out, his eyes stunned closed, and his skin a pale yellow.

When I told a writing group in Taos about abstract statements, Judy, a writer in the class, let out a shriek of glee. "Oh, I get it! Thirty-six details equal one cosmic statement. We can make a game like Monopoly. Detail cards: shoe, gum, horse, toenail. Cosmic cards: I hate you, God is love, Truth is beautiful. It is a perfect Santa Fe game. They'd have to shut up until they made some grounded statements."

Sometimes, however, abstract statements are not abstract.

They are solid thoughts. They come from the bottom of the mind and have their own concreteness. You discover these as you write. They are not vague or mushy. These kinds of statements are as solid as rocks, though there is no visual picture to go with them. They are true and hold their own integrity. Good philosophy should be based on them; good religion, too. I cannot in this moment think of an example, but as you write, when you contact them, you know it, your body feels it. They echo through your whole being. They are as solid as bread and hold the reader's attention as well as if they were a good story.

Try this:

Either by yourself or with a partner list five abstract statements. Try some simple ones, too, like "Thank you," "I'm sorry." Now back each one up with at least a paragraph of solid, concrete details. Try even giving thirty-six, as Judy advises. Here you have the abstract statement first.

Now switch. Describe a situation in detail and then take a leap into a cosmic statement.

There are lots of possibilities here. Have fun.

54

Procrastination and Waiting

*T*here is a difference between procrastination and waiting. Procrastination is pushing aside or putting off writing. It is thinking the moment is tomorrow. It is a way not to let in vital energy. Don't procrastinate. Write now.

Waiting is something full-bodied. Perhaps waiting isn't even a good word for it. *Pregnant* is better. You've worked on something for a while. You are excited by it, even happy, but you are wise and step back. You take a walk, but this walk isn't to avoid the writing on your desk. It is a walk full of your writing. It is also full of the trees you pass, the river, the sky. You are letting writing work on you.

Procrastination is a cutting off. It diminishes you.

Waiting is when you are already in the work and you are feeding it and being fed by it. Then you can trust the waiting.

Do not use the excuse of "waiting" for the right idea or story in order to begin. That is procrastination. Get to work.

Know the difference between the two. Do not fool yourself. Be tough. But be tough the way a blade of grass is: rooted, willing to lean, and at peace with what's around it.

55

Verbs

I am amazed by the power of verbs. They carry the energy for a sentence. They are the action. Think of sentences without them: Vivian a tire onto the rack; Fido a lamb chop. Verbs are the stars that light up the dark sky: Vivian *hoisted* a tire onto the rack. Fido *devoured* a lamb chop. They are the joint that moves the sentence, like the elbow that connects the upper and lower arm.

I fooled around a lot with verbs when I began the novel. I was placing my characters in time and I had to figure out what kind of time. I decided to cut the fat away from verbs as much as possible and let them be immediate and exposed. I tried to stay in present time as much as possible, even if it was simple past present time. It made the writing alive. It reined in the wild horses of the mind that got lost in the "had been gone," "having had been gone," "would be gone" and instead simply stated "she went." I learned that "she was sick" carried the movement forward better than "she had been sick." I kept the verbs as simple as possible. "Nell would go to the store, so she would avoid her mother." Using the conditional tense here moves the action away from us. Using *would be* makes it for all time, continually, and that is a generalization. Nothing is for all time. It is better to capture the one moment, and if that is strong the reader will carry it inside him or her. Try "Nell went to the store. She avoided her mother." Much simpler.

Changing the verb tense can change the whole tone of the piece. A friend gave me her manuscript to read. In one paragraph I wrote "WOW!" in the margin. What I meant was "You're going for your father's throat here." When we went over the passage, I asked her if she was sure she wanted to keep it as is. I thought she was brave and a tiny bit off.

Here is her first version: "Being with my father after my performance was not a way to care for myself. The talk *would be* about baseball games, his next visit to India, frequent-flyer miles on United. It *would be* as if the performance had never happened and I was not present."

I liked the original detail, but the two underlined verbs created condemnation and made me squirm. I suggested she change "would be" to "was," simple past. Look how it lightened the load for everyone: "Being with my father after my performance was not a way to care for myself. The talk *was* about baseball games, his next visit to India, frequent-flyer miles on United. It *was* as if the performance had never happened and I was not present."

Can you feel the difference? The father isn't frozen in that action forever, and it frees the writer to see and deal with her father in the moment. She is not caught in the web of prejudgments. It is better to stay with original detail when there is anger, because after your anger has passed, the writing will still carry the dignity of the insight. It simply did happen this way. It was the truth.

56

Whales

I began my novel at the Pink Adobe Bar one August afternoon three and a half years ago. I sat at a small wooden table by the window, sipped at a Perrier, and told the waiter I did not want a bowl of salty popcorn. I leaned over the notebook and began to write. I wrote about a cremation on a mesa. Sunflowers grew tall outside the window where I sat.

This past Saturday night, I went back to the Pink Adobe with Margarite to toast the completion of the novel and help cut its ties with my life.

Margarite said to me, "You know, when you returned to New Mexico, it haunted me. We both had our first books of poetry come out at the same time years ago—you in Minnesota and me in New Mexico. But nothing happened with my book. It caused no ripples; it didn't change the world. I took it as a message. I wanted to do something, so I became a Jungian analyst. You came back to New Mexico all gung-ho, like poetry mattered."

"Yeah, well, I was in Minnesota where there's a lot of hullabaloo about writing. If I'd started out here, I probably would have become a therapist, too," I told her.

Instead, returning to New Mexico after six years in Minnesota really got me going. Because there were no seminars, grants, workshops in New Mexico to tell me I was a writer, the only thing that made me one was the act of writing. I was so scared not to be a writer that I wrote all the time.

After I finished the novel, I flew to La Paz, Mexico, and got on a boat for a week to follow the blue whales. They are the biggest animals that ever lived. Their hearts are the size of a Volkswagen bug. They weigh a hundred tons. An average elephant weighs six tons. Their penises are nine to twelve feet long.

After the marine biologist gave a lecture one night on the boat, I was quiet and then raised my hand. "You mean, they swim all their lives?" I said in wonder. People around me laughed. I asked such an obvious question. They didn't understand that I wanted to intuit the dream, called life, of a whale.

I realize now why I went to see them. A novel is a big dream, a whale of a dream. You have to go under for a long time into the dark waters of the mind and stay there. After I finished the novel, I wanted to nod to the blue whales and say, "I've been there, too. I understand."

Poetry, which I wrote for thirteen years, was easier. I could go under and pop back up. With a novel, I had to stay down there. I had to tell a story. It had to connect from one time I wrote to another time. I had to leave myself, my will and control, and let the story come through me. I had to become egoless.

For all the years I sat *zazen*, there was a place I came up against, became frightened of, and moved away from. That place was simply being there with my breath, my legs crossed, and my hands on my knees for endless hours of sitting meditation. I was afraid of that egoless state where nothing was happening. I thought I existed only when I created activities, universes, dreams. In the novel, the writer stops existing. She gives her life over so her characters speak through her. We are not used to that egoless state. It is scary.

It's a lot like the experience of being in therapy. Suddenly, there's nothing much to discuss and you notice. "Uh-oh, it's me and the therapist, another human being facing me in this room." So you get nervous and jump in with, "You know, I think I forgot to tell you something about my mother's dress." We make up anything so we don't just have to be there face-to-face.

I was so excited about telling Margarite all this that I ordered a lamb chop dinner, even though it was nine-thirty and I had already eaten dinner.

Margarite said, "I have a lucrative therapy practice now and I realize I must write. I can't run from it anymore."

I smiled. "Sometimes we make side dances before we plunge in. I've know several women who became therapists but wanted to be writers. I don't blame you. Maybe I'll become a therapist, too. At least there's another person, in the flesh, who talks back to you." I smiled. "I'll do straight Freudian analysis. Everyone will have an Eddy-puss complex."

Margarite told me that she is afraid to let out what she has begun to write now. She's afraid to expose how she really thinks and feels.

I told Margarite, "I think everyone feels afraid with their first book." I paused. "And their second book and their third and their fourth . . ."

The problem is that there are no good maps for the journey

of a writer; each one goes it alone. Ultimately, that is always true, but it would be good to hear accounts of the process, so we know others have walked the path. We, as writers, need to legitimize our way as a path that we have taken. Instead, a lot of writers act like victims plagued by the agonies of writing. We are actually great warriors facing the barriers to truth. We are digesting experience for society.

The last month that I was finishing *Banana Rose*, I was angry all the time. I couldn't understand it because I thought I should be happy.

I called Kate and told her.

She said, "Oh, yeah, you're finishing a novel. The two I wrote—when I came to the end—I was furious all the time."

She didn't have an explanation for the anger, but hearing that she too had gone through it helped. I let myself be mad and kept on writing.

Anger is an emotion that demands motion, change. The energy of anger pushed me through. But I think the anger was also the beginning of my grief. This load I carried that I had learned to love and hate, was involved in, was coming to an end. I could go to the corner store now and buy potato chips, and there would be just that act: holding the bag, exchanging the coins, hearing the cash register ring. While I worked on the novel, my characters, who had become my darlings, were with me. Maybe in the next chapter Anna would want to buy potato chips? While I wrote the novel, my simple world resounded: I was connected with other beings I held inside me. After the novel, it was only me again, alone in the world. A life I held dear, the life of the novel, was over.

57

Keep Writing

I thought I'd experience great relief when *Banana Rose* was completed. Instead I found myself wandering around Santa Fe feeling lost and missing Nell Schwartz, the main character, very much. I realized that my closest relationship was with a person who didn't exist and now she was gone. It felt as though I'd dragged my darling Nell on my back over the Himalayas for twenty years with just a heel of bread to eat once a week, no shoes, a thin cotton sweater, no compass, no direction, and when I got her to safety at the end, I just waved *adios* and she was gone forever from my life. Some gratitude!

One morning I woke up and thought, "Wait a minute! When did you decide to be a writer? I don't think you ever figured this out clearly. Characters you love leave you! I'm going for some career counseling. It might not be the best decision. After all, I'm older now. I didn't consider retirement, social security, vacation benefits, my life! How did I get into this anyway?"

About ten years ago, I knew I had two choices: Either I was going to become a Zen priest or a writer. I opted for writer. I thought it would be easier. I hadn't written a novel then. Now I want to stand up at my writing workshops, throw up my hands, and say, "Listen, get out while you can. Run, you'll be reimbursed at the door." "That's how I'll save the world," I think to myself. "Then I'll become a computer programmer or a short-order cook in a café in Kansas."

Two years ago, I was at a dinner party with old friends in Minneapolis. I was at the head of the table. On either side of me were two women who had just had their first novels published. Pat Francisco worked on *Cold Feet* (Simon & Schuster, 1988) for eight years. I said to both of them—I'd been working on *Banana Rose* for a year and a half at that time— "Why didn't you warn me? Why didn't you tell me it was so hard?"

They both grimaced, nodded, and were wordless. There was nothing to say. It hurt.

Meanwhile, in the face of this agony of a finished novel, I notice I am casting around for material for my next book. I was on a massage table a week ago when the masseuse and I discovered we were brought up two towns apart on Long Island. She said, "Remember Jolly Roger's?" It was a small amusement park with a restaurant attached that parents took their kids to on Hempstead Turnpike. She said, "Jolly Roger's," and all of it sprang up in my face. The Cadillac dealership on the corner, the humidity, Bethpage State Park, the split-level development, the mailbox, curb, overcast sky, blue Buick, the bakery next to May's department store. Ah-ha! my next novel would take place there—on mythical Long Island five million lifetimes from where I am now.

It's funny how we work. Part of me is ranting and raving about a new career—as though I had an old one, writing is no career to begin with—and meanwhile, another part of me is dragging her feet in the dark waters, looking for some old dead fish floating about that she can breathe life into and dream up a story about.

I had dinner last night at the Zia Diner with Pam, a friend who had just finished a novel. I was telling her about my idea for a career change and she said, "Huh, I know I'll keep writing book after book. That's no problem. My problem is how will I make enough money to support myself while I write?"

I realized if it isn't one thing, it's another. Right now I have enough money to live on, so the problem becomes the pain of writing. If I had no money, the problem would be the pain of poverty and writing would be the promised land.

Well, we all know the moral of this story, don't we? Shut up and write anyway. Don't use anything as an excuse.

58

Months Later

After I finished the novel, I asked Kate, "Now what do I do?"

"Get three novelists to read it and listen to what they have to say. I'll read it. I'm sure Mary Logue and Pat will read it."

I gave the manuscript to Kate. I took a long time to ask Mary and Pat. I was timid. After all, I was asking them to read five hundred pages. I waited nine months before I got together with them.

I finally got up the courage to meet with Mary. She said to cut out the first eighty pages. "Just jump into the action. And here, get rid of the middle hundred and fifty pages where Nell wanders around." I nodded. If it were eight months earlier, I would have grabbed the manuscript off the table and run out of the house, sobbing. Instead, I agreed with her. She explained to me that there has to be at least one question that makes the reader turn the pages to find out the answer.

"The chapters should move the question forward," she

told me. "If a chapter digresses, you should know you've decided to digress with that chapter."

Again I nodded. "So the question is sort of the backbone of the book? What's the question here?" I pointed to the manuscript on the table.

"We want to know if Nell ends up with Gauguin."

"You're kidding! So mundane? Whenever anyone asks me what the book is about, I always wax philosophical, tell them it's about the hippie years and after, about a generation."

Mary laughed. "Nope. I want to know what happens to Nell and Gauguin. The background is the hippie years."

I took her out for dinner that night. She had been so kind and I appreciated it.

A week later, I sat catty-corner to Pat at her dining room table. It was snowing outside.

Pat went on about how beautiful the writing was, how she loved the characters and cared about them, how she found herself often laughing aloud, but—and I was waiting for this "but"—"Nat, it's plotless." She lifted her shoulders. "There's no plot!" She said "plot" as though the word had three syllables.

I burst out laughing. "You know, I was getting that feeling."

I paused. "Pat, what is plot anyway?" It took me three and a half years and many pages to ask that essential question.

"Well, E. M. Forster wrote that a story is: The king died, the queen died. A plot is: The king died, the queen died of grief."

I'd heard that before, but I didn't understand it until now. Plot is about cause and effect, about karma. If something happens, there is a result. If all the other chapters lead to the result, we feel satisfied because it resonates with what we innately know to be true.

Story is what kids tell us. "This happened and then this happened, then this happened." We've all heard them trail on with an endless tale with no structure. Plot echoes a structure or a design to the universe—cause and effect, karma.

Pat showed me different ways I could create tension and develop some scenes and ax out others. She, too, was very kind. I find that writers who are really working are kind. They know what writing is about, how hard it is. They have compassion.

I called Kate after I left Pat's. "Kate, Pat said the novel's plotless." I laughed.

Kate said, "Well, of course it's plotless. It's about your life."

I called Jonathon, my agent, and told him.

He responded, "If you want to go nowhere, read *Banana Rose*. If you can't tell the difference between sleeping, eating a grilled cheese sandwich, or watching television, then you are reading Nat's novel."

We both laughed. Then he started to defend me. "Well, I don't like plots anyway. Aren't plots very un-Zen-like?"

Two months later, I was walking through the streets of Santa Fe with Greg Brown, a fine songwriter. He was visiting from Iowa. I was telling him about my plotless novel.

He said, "Who needs plot. If a writer wins me over, I'll go anyplace with them."

"No, it isn't about that. I want to learn what plot is. I want to learn it all. I can let go of plot, only after I know it."

We were walking across the New Mexico Federal parking lot. I was looking at my feet and the slate blue pavement. It was then that I first articulated why I really wrote the novel. "I wanted to learn what prose had to teach me. I was a poet for thirteen years. I wanted my body to know the ordinariness of laying down one sentence after another." I was motioning with my left hand. My right hand was carrying the leather briefcase my sister gave me for my fortieth birthday. It held chapters for *Wild Mind*. "I wanted to learn how to write a complete sentence. I'd been writing in phrases for so long. Like laying concrete, I wanted that steadiness. Work. One day after the other. My body wanted to develop that. I wanted to be steady on the earth. It was hard." I shook my head.

I had lunch with Kate last week. She said, "What's happening with *Banana Rose*?"

"You know, Kate, part of me wants to forget it. I want to go on with my good life. It was so hard."

"Nat, I believe in it. You can't leave it."

Kate's right. Last night I took a walk in the moonlight on the mesa. Nell appeared with a whole new ending. She was full of energy. She was way ahead of me, driving up to Denver to save an old friend. I called after her, "I'm coming, Nell, I'm coming."

59

Failure

I met my editor at Bantam last month. I signed the contract to write *Wild Mind* over a year ago, but I had only spoken to the editor on the phone; I'd never met her.

As we talked, sitting in her office on the twenty-fifth floor above Fifth Avenue, I felt I could be who I was with her.

After about a half hour, I bent closer. "Toni, I have something to tell you. I couldn't tell you when I signed the contract because I didn't know how the writing would go and I supposed you wouldn't have thought it was a very good attitude, but I said to myself, 'Don't worry, Nat, I give you full permission to completely fail. You don't have to live up to anyone. So what if everyone loved *Bones*? You can now write a book they hate. You are completely free!'

"Now that the book is going well, I can tell you this pledge I made to myself."

She nodded. "I understand. That's great. As the representative of a publishing company, I want a writer to write a second book to build on the first, but sometimes the writer is not ready. As an editor for writers, I want to tell them to lie fallow for a while." She paused. "You should put what you just told me in your book."

It was important to give myself permission to fail. It is the only way to write. We can't live up to anyone's high standards, including our own.

A student asked me about this in a workshop recently, and I wanted to help her understand where I got this attitude. How was I so smart not to be intimidated by my success with *Bones*? I'm not usually so smart in other areas of my life.

I closed my eyes, became still and tried to go all the way back to the beginning. I opened my eyes. I told her, "Kindness. It stemmed from kindness. I have always been kind to myself in the area of writing. I know if I'm not kind, if I get too tough, I'll get scared, close up, freeze."

Failure is a hard word for people to take. Use the word kindness then instead. Let yourself be kind. And this kindness comes from an understanding of what it is to be a human being. Have compassion for yourself when you write. There is no failure—just a big field to wander in.

60

Lazy

I was broke the spring I was finishing *Writing Down the Bones*. In order to alleviate my worry and to encourage my writing, I signed a contract to teach fifth and sixth grade in a private school the following September. I said to myself, "Don't worry, Nat. By the time September comes around, you'll be done with your book, you'll have sold it, and you won't have to teach, but it's a little security to let you rest at ease. Now get to work. Finish that book."

September came. The book was done but wasn't sold. I had to take the job. I hadn't had a full-time job in years, much less being the teacher for twenty-five eleven- and twelve-year-olds. I was in charge of their math, their science, their rubber boots, their mittens. It was ridiculous.

Friends from out of town who only knew me as a writer kept asking, "Now exactly what are you doing? Math? Nat! Math?"

When Kate visited me for the first time in Santa Fe, I asked her, "Well, what do you want to see?"

She crossed her arms. "I want to see you in the classroom. I want to see just what you're doing."

Later, she said, "Not bad. Those fifth- and sixth-graders have never seen anything like it. You're teaching the Holocaust and Elvis all in the same day."

I smiled. "Well, I figured I'd better teach what I know."

At three o'clock each day, when school was over, I drove home, walked into the house, grabbed my notebook, and walked directly to the Galisteo Newsstand. I had an exact route I walked each time: half down Galisteo Street, half through the weeds of a deserted lot. I ordered my hot chocolate. I sat down. I opened my notebook and I said, "Go." I wrote for two hours.

By the time I returned to the classroom the next day, I could hardly remember the kids' names. Sometimes eight of them would be hanging on me first thing in the morning, all at the same time. "Natalie, Natalie," they'd say. They all had something to tell me.

I'd say, "I just changed my name last night and I'm not telling you what it is." It was a stressful year.

Stress is basically a disconnection from the earth, a forgetting of the breath. I had too many things to do when I taught, and I felt the tension between those responsibilities and wanting to write. My time was diced up into minutes and hours rather than into seasons and the movement of the moon and sun. Stress is an ignorant state. It believes that everything is an emergency. Nothing is that important. Just lie down.

All writers have a natural bent toward laziness. That is good. Utilize it. The couch is a good place. Lie there for a whole day in the middle of everything. It is like waiting for vinegar to settle after you shake it up with oil. Let the oil get clear again. You get clear. This is a very wholesome place to write from. It brings you back to remembering the essentials: sky out the window, feet on a cushion, ceiling above your head, ground below.

My friend Geneen called this morning. She'd just been on a book tour. She was frantic; she couldn't get on another plane to visit me. We had planned to go on a writing retreat together. She said maybe she should drive to a summer resort in Carmel Valley for a few days.

I said, "Do me a favor. Just stop. Don't go anyplace else. Just lie down for the rest of the day."

"Lie down?" she said.

"Yeah, just lie down. Hang out. Don't go anyplace for two full days. Clip your toenails. Spend hours on the couch. Just let it all lie. Don't do anything."

"You're kidding."

"Geneen, you don't know the essential ingredient of writing: laziness. In this society, we have to learn to nurture it. Just lie around. What did you think? You'd come to New Mexico and attack the page? Lie down. Trust it."

Writing is at the bottom of our life. After you're cleared from lying around, your desire to write will rise up to the surface like a bubble or an old dead fish. Then you can get up for no reason and write a little. The writing will not be full of aggression. You will not be trying to prove yourself. You'll just set down one word after another. It will be good. Trust me.

Try this:

Put aside one day a month to do nothing. No, not an hour or the late afternoon, but the whole day. Just lie around. Don't jog, don't cook.

I know, I know, some of you have kids, responsibilities, but surely you can find one day, if not a day a month, then how about one day in your whole life? Take one of them and be completely lazy. You don't have to dress if you don't want. Don't bother to brush your teeth; it's always such a bother. Let things be.

At the end of the day, sidle over to your notebook, but only if you feel like it, and write. If you don't write, it's okay too. The benefits of a lazy day will feed your writing for a long time.

I am not going to give you any other instructions. Be lazy and it will be enough.

61

Lost

*M*iriam and I were driving up to the Japanese hot tubs on Hyde Park Road. We were climbing a steep hill as I told her, "My B.A. and M.A. don't mean anything to me. I never used them; they never brought me one inch closer to writing one good line. If I had them right here, I'd tear them up, open this window and make confetti of them. We could watch 'em blow down the hill."

"What about your teaching certificate? You're always proud of that," she chimed in.

"Yes, I am. That's technical. I could do something with it." I nodded. We were turning a wide curve. "I was thinking the other day, if I had kids, I wouldn't give them one cent to go to college. College was stupid, absolutely stupid. But a technical school"—I took my hand off the steering wheel—"I'd send them there. They could learn to do something."

I sounded like a raving redneck, but I couldn't help it. I

was raving against all the dead hours I had wasted in class-rooms. Then I went on to harangue about institutions.

"I don't believe in institutions, either. They take energy and freeze it. Something that used to be alive becomes dead. Look at the early years of Zen centers, and now look at them. Look at co-ops and natural foods. Now natural foods are all packaged at the supermarkets. Public schools. They can't die. They keep getting funded forever. If something can't die, it's not alive. Kids are dying in those classrooms. There's no vitality."

"What about the public libraries?" Miriam has this annoy-ing habit of trying to be logical. "And museums?"

"Well, I do love libraries, though the truth is I never go in them. Give me a bookstore and a café. But libraries house something that is alive—a good book—and make it available. You can take a book home. But I don't know about museums. Some of them, I've had to keep myself from collapsing—they put me to sleep." Then I hesitated. I'd seen some great exhibits lately, but there were so many years as a kid I felt dead boredom in them.

That night I went to hear a lecture on divorce by a famous speaker who had his beginnings in the twelve-step Alcoholics Anonymous program.

When I found out the tickets were twenty-five dollars apiece, I told Eddie, "Hey, let's not go. That's ridiculous."

"Oh, c'mon," he said. "It's a cultural phenomenon we're going to see."

I conceded. I was always interested in cultural movements.

We got there early and waited in the lobby. They were setting up video equipment and wouldn't let us into the auditorium. As we waited, we tried to name other times we'd spent twenty-five dollars on a ticket.

"Dylan was twenty dollars," I said.

Mary said, "I spent fifty dollars for Broadway."

"Yeah!" I lit up. "I spent about that much to see Lily Tomlin—it was worth it!"

When they finally opened the doors, we dashed in and got front-row seats. The tickets said there would be live music. I wondered how they would combine that with the lecture on divorce. The man came out and was deep into his talk when all the electricity went out at the Lensic Theatre.

Eddie, who used to be an electrician, said, "This always happens here. We told them ten years ago that they needed to put in six or seven thousand dollars to update their equipment. They wouldn't do it."

As the lights went out, the speaker was telling us a story about a divorced minister who slept around. He continued to talk in the dark and told us the whole story. Then he switched to questions and answers for about a half hour while the electricity was worked on. Someone held up a flashlight to see raised hands in the audience. The lights still did not go on, so we took a break.

I was naïve and did not understand why he continued with questions and answers after the break until the lights went on. If he could answer questions, why not just continue talking? An hour had passed. In answer to one question, he got personal about his own father and I was touched. I thought, "This is what made him famous." Suddenly, all the lights flared on.

He said quickly, "I'm going to have to tell that last story over."

The camera turned on him and he launched into a complete retelling of the story about the minister who slept around. I suddenly realized that everything had to do with the filming—that's why he did questions and answers when the lights went out. He couldn't continue his talk in the dark because it couldn't be videotaped. I had naïvely thought he was talking to us; I'd even paid twenty-five dollars to see him. I looked around at the audience as he told the story we had already heard, and there was a look of innocent betrayal in their eyes. Some mouths were even hanging open. We'd heard this story. We didn't matter. Only the video mattered.

He lost me after that. I didn't believe a word he said. Then, near the end, he misquoted Buddha, saying for some reason we all have to suffer to learn and then he said Buddha said, "Life is suffering." Yes, Buddha did say that, but it did not mean what this man said it did. I felt a slow fury.

Eddie was right. We went to see a cultural phenomenon. Someone starts out in a twelve-step program where there are no dues and fees, gets help, becomes a dynamic speaker on its behalf, and makes it into a business. Then the business takes priority and the person again disconnects from himself. This time not because of alcohol but because of money or success. I was watching a man divided from himself. The man on stage had become an institution.

This can happen to a writer, too. Do not freeze with something you have written. Go on and write something else. If you are a writer, your business is to write. It is what keeps us honest. If you have just finished a novel and feel exhausted and do not want to begin another big project, then just do writing practice several times a week to keep the energy moving. Do not freeze with your work. After you have finished a piece of work, the work is then none of your business. Go on and do something else.

62

For Everyone

*F*rances is living in Santa Fe. One week ago, she came up to Taos to visit me on the mesa. It was a beautiful, still day. I made a healthy delicious dinner: fried tofu, brown and wild rice with mushrooms, and steamed broccoli. Frances said the broccoli was her favorite. After the meal, we sipped tea.

"Do you want to smoke some marijuana?" she asked.

"I don't think I have any. Let's look in my drug bag," I jokingly said. I pulled out a plastic bag I kept in the refrigerator. In it were one or two old peyote buttons, psychedelic mushrooms that were so old they turned to ash when I touched them. Friends passed through and left me these as gifts. I rarely used anything. I just put them in my "drug bag." I put the bag on the kitchen table.

"Hey, there's that tab of Ecstasy I gave you two years ago," Frances said and pointed.

"Oh, you gave me that? I forgot." I suddenly smiled. "Let's take it now."

We dissolved it in a glass of grape juice and each of us drank half. Then we took a short walk on the mesa. We didn't feel anything. We took it on full stomachs, and the capsule, after all, was two years old. We walked back to the house.

I turned to Frances. "I feel a tingling in my right foot."

"From what?" she asked.

"Maybe the stuff?"

She shrugged doubtfully.

I heard the phone ring as we neared the house. I ran to get it. It was Melanie in Minneapolis. Roshi had gone into the hospital again. He had an infection, and his last chemotherapy was due next week. I hung up, went over to my desk, and lit a long stick of incense that I had from Eiheiji monastery, where Dogen is buried in Japan.

I closed my eyes. "Be well, old friend." I looked at Roshi's picture I had hanging from a tack on my wooden book shelf, and I bowed.

Frances and I then got towels and drove to a hot springs I knew about on the Rio Grande. We were chewing gum, and as we neared Arroyo Hondo we chewed hard and fast. The Ecstasy tab was having its effect. A slip of the moon had risen and lit our way as we climbed down a narrow path through the black rocks of the Rio Grande gorge.

Frances and I took off our clothes and climbed into the hot pool that was right next to the fast-moving river. We didn't talk. A man came down, took off his clothes, and from a distance I could see he had long hair and many tattoos. "Uh-oh, a biker," I thought and panicked. Then he came nearer and I relaxed immediately. I knew he was a holy man. I could feel it. He lowered himself into the pool.

"From Taos?" he asked us.

I nodded.

"I came down from South Dakota to lead the Sun Dance that's in a few days. You know the Sun Dance?" he asked.

"A little," I said.

He pointed to his breasts. There were scars there. "The men hang themselves from here," he pointed again to the scars, "so we can feel the pain of women in childbirth and so we can go into the next life scarred as we are scarring the earth and using all her wood. This is the time when Indians mate to have children. It is the time wolves and buffalo mate." He went on to tell us how he fought in Korea. Mostly I felt his presence. It was the way I felt around Roshi.

Frances and I got out of the pool, dried ourselves and climbed a cliff, crouched side by side, and watched the moonlit river for a long time. I felt sorrow inside me and knew it would always be there.

Frances turned suddenly and said, "Name one positive thing your father gave you."

I was silent for a moment. "He gave me my life." I nodded slowly.

Today is Saturday. It is the last day of Sun Dance. They have been dancing now for five days. I have been invited to attend today. I feel honored and split. Split because I haven't written in a long while and I need to. I decide to go instead to a café on the plaza and write. I honor everything that is going on at the dances, but writing for long hours today is my way to become present. As I write, I feel their dance, the day, the sun. I am alone here, but I write for everyone.

Jack Kornfield, a *vipassana* meditation teacher, said last week up at Lama, "You meditate *by* yourself but not *for* yourself. You meditate *for* everyone."

This is how we should write.

About the Author

NATALIE GOLDBERG is a writer and teacher. She lives in northern New Mexico.